The Reminiscences of
John W. Reagan
Member of the Golden Thirteen

Interviewed by
Paul Stillwell

U.S. Naval Institute
Annapolis, Maryland
Copyright ©1991

Preface

In the first few months of 1944, 16 black enlisted men went through officer training at Great Lakes, Illinois. Of the group, 12 were commissioned as ensigns and one as a warrant officer. They were the Navy's first black officers. Collectively, the group has come to be known as the Golden Thirteen. In the autumn of 1986, the Naval Institute began an oral history project involving the eight surviving members of the group. This volume represents the life story of one of those eight men, John Reagan.

Reagan was one of several top-flight athletes in the Golden Thirteen. He particularly excelled in football and wrestling. He was so capable that when he finished his college studies in 1947, he was offered contracts to play professional football in both the United States and Canada. He played one season for the Winnipeg Blue Bombers of the Canadian Football League. He has also been an excellent leader, both in the Navy and in his civilian career. When he was in service school at Hampton, Virginia, he was chosen for a leadership role within the battalion of enlisted men. His success in that assignment led, in turn, to his selection for the first class of black officer candidates.

As an officer, John Reagan faced the same disappointment as the other members of the Golden Thirteen. They were not given assignments commensurate with their abilities. Whereas he had hoped to go aboard a combatant ship and become a division officer, Reagan served instead in a patrol craft, yard tugboat, and a cargo-handling battalion overseas. In 1949, he was recalled to active duty to aid in minority recruiting, and stayed on for the duration of the Korean War. He wound up in an amphibious boat unit operating first in California and later in Japan. It was interesting work and brought him closer to the real Navy than he had been during World War II. While in that unit, he was chosen executive officer, a tribute to his leadership and administrative abilities. Of the Golden Thirteen, Reagan probably spent more time on active duty than anyone except Dennis Nelson, who served until retirement.

In civilian life, Reagan has worked in the state government, the field of real estate, and in developing innovative programs on behalf of the Urban League. Operating particularly in the southern California area, he has sought ways to help America's black citizens become better educated, better trained for job opportunities, and more a part of the nation's economic life. His biggest disappointment along the way was the loss of his only son, John W. "Skip" Reagan, Jr. Skip served one hitch in the Navy, later enlisted in the Marine Corps, and was killed in Vietnam. For a father who hoped to turn his business over to his son, it was a terrible blow.

In the transcript that follows, both the interviewer and the interviewee have done some editing in the interests of clarity, accuracy, and brevity. The original verbatim transcript is on file with the Naval Institute. The transcription was done by Ms. Deborah Reid and Ms. Joanne Patmore of the Naval Institute's oral history staff. Ms. Linda O'Doughda and I compiled the subject index at the back of the volume.

                                        Paul Stillwell
                                        Director of Oral History
                                        U.S. Naval Institute
                                        January 1991

JOHN WALTER REAGAN

Born on 5 March 1920 in Marshall (Harrison County), Texas, to John Llwellyn and Bernice Bonita (Ector) Reagan.

A graduate of Copernicus Grammar School (1935) and Lindblom High School (1939) in Chicago, Illinois, he won city and state wrestling championships and letters in football, track, and boxing, along with scholastic honors.

Reagan entered Montana State University, Missoula, on a scholarship in September 1939. Because of the imminent prospect of military service, he did not return after the fall semester in 1941. Reagan signed up for the Army Air Forces after Pearl Harbor, but his orders came too late. He had enlisted in the U.S. Navy in July 1942 as apprentice seaman. Recruit training was held at Great Lakes, and he enrolled in electrical school at Hampton, Virginia, graduating Electrician's Mate Third Class in December 1942.

Reagan served in the auxiliary minesweeper USS Firefly out of Point Loma, California, until ordered to Norfolk in the fall to 1943 to serve in a destroyer as a an electrician's mate second class. Before reporting aboard, he was ordered to Great Lakes to Officer Candidate School, one of what became known as the Golden Thirteen.

Reagan was commissioned an ensign, U.S. Naval Reserve, on 17 March 1944. He subsequently served as officer in charge of the electrical course at Naval Training School, Hampton, Virginia; on board patrol craft and a yard tug; the Eastern Sea Frontier; and in a Logistic Support Company in Guam and Okinawa at war's end. In January 1946, he was released to inactive duty.

Reagan then completed college at Montana State University in June 1947. He played professional football for the Winnipeg Blue Bombers in Manitoba, Canada, for one season. The Navy asked him to return to active duty in October 1949. He assisted in minority recruiting out of New York Naval Recruiting headquarters. Reagan was promoted to lieutenant in April 1950.

He went on to serve as executive officer of Boat Unit One in Japan from mid-1953 to 1954 when he was released once more to inactive duty. Reagan went on to serve in active training units several years and was promoted to lieutenant commander in the early 1960s.

His principal occupation in retirement has been as a real estate broker and investor. He has three daughters--Kathy, Bernida, and Penny--living in the Los Angeles area. His only son, John Reagan, Jr., was killed in action in Vietnam.

Reagan currently resides in Encinitas, California, with his wife, Willita (Dede).

Chronological Transcript of Service

July 1942	Enlisted in U.S. Navy, apprentice seaman, recruit training command, Great Lakes, Illinois
December 1942	Class "A" Electrical School, Hampton, Virginia
1943	EM3-EM2, Auxiliary Minesweeper, Point Loma, California
1943-1944	EM1 and Officer Candidate School, Great Lakes, Illinois
17 March 1944	Commissioned an ensign, Great Lakes, Illinois
1944 - 1945	Subchaser and yard tugboat, Third Naval District, New York, New York
1945	Operations Officer, Logistics Support Company, Guam and Okinawa
January 1946	Released to inactive duty as a lieutenant (junior grade)
October 1949	Returned to active duty
1952	Assistant to officer in charge, U.S. Navy Recruiting, New York, New York

1953-54   Executive officer, Boat Unit One,
                        Yokosuka, Japan (promoted to lieutenant
                        commander)

January 1954   Released to inactive duty

Education

Bachelor of Arts from Montana State University in economics and sociology; graduate studies at the University of Southern California in public administration.

Civilian Employment

Associate Broker and Senior Investment Consultant, C-21, in San Diego, California

President and Director of Counseling, Community Housing Services, Pasadena, California

Professional Associations and Licenses

Licensed real estate broker in California
Member of the National Federation of Housing Counselors

Civic Activities

President, Board of Governors, Pasadena/Foothill Branch, Los
    Angeles Urban League, 1977
President, Bunker Hill Democratic Club, Los Angeles
Elected member, Los Angeles County Democratic Central
    Committee

Authorization

The U. S. Naval Institute is hereby authorized to make available to individuals, libraries, and other repositories of its choosing the transcripts of two oral history interviews concerning the life and career of the undersigned. The interviews were recorded on 15 January 1987 and 10 April 1989, in collaboration with Paul Stillwell for the U.S. Naval Institute.

The undersigned does hereby release and assign to the U.S. Naval Institute all right, title, restrictions, and interest in the interviews. The copyright in both the oral and transcribed versions shall be the sole property of the U.S. Naval Institute. The tape recordings of the interviews are and will remain the property of the U.S. Naval Institute.

Signed and sealed this _____ day of May 1989.

Mr. John Reagan

J. W. Reagan #1 - 1

Interview Number 1 with Mr. John W. Reagan
Place: Mr. Reagan's home in Encinitas, California
Date: Thursday, 15 January 1987
Interviewer: Paul Stillwell

Q: It's a real pleasure to see you. I've seen the other seven so far who are still alive, and I sense a feeling of family among the group of you, all these years later.

Mr. Reagan: There's no question about it.

Q: Because there was a very tight bond formed in undergoing the training together.

Mr. Reagan: Yes.

Q: One thing that I've done with the other seven that has been interesting is not only to discuss the naval training, but the period of life before and after, to establish some background for the individuals that form the group. So why don't we go back to the beginning and some of your earliest memories. Where and when were you born, and what are some of your childhood memories?

Mr. Reagan: I was born in Marshall, Texas, a long time ago, 1920.

Q: The same time as Frank Sublett, in fact.*

Mr. Reagan: It's a funny thing. Sublett and I found out that we were born on the same month, same day, same year. We're the two youngest guys in the group.

Anyway, the earliest period I remember is after we had moved to Shreveport, Louisiana, and I guess we were there until I was about five or six. Our dad had gone north to Chicago to try and better himself.**

Q: What sort of work did he do?

Mr. Reagan: He was a kind of a jack-of-all-trades, very mechanically inclined. So we joined him in Chicago. We left Chicago after a while during the Depression and went to Flint, Michigan, where he worked for Buick Company.

Q: How much memory do you have of the time in Texas and Louisiana?

Mr. Reagan: As a child, not a great deal. I remember running around in the country all the time, climbing trees, riding horses. I had one uncle who was a cattle grower,

---
*Frank Ellis Sublett, Jr., is a member of the Golden Thirteen. His oral history is in the Naval Institute collection.
**His father was John Llewllyn Reagan.

J. W. Reagan #1 - 3

and I used to watch him slay the cattle and things like that. Then after we went away, I'd visit periodically, and I remember the cotton farms, picking the cotton, taking it to the gin, and things like that. But in the early part of it, I don't remember a great deal about Texas and Louisiana.

Q: How well did your family fare during the Depression? Did your father finally find steady work?

Mr. Reagan: Oh, my dad always worked, and he'd work on more than one job. He hated relief. He always cared for us well. There were two or three separations from time to time, mainly because my mother wanted to work too.* She wanted to do things and have things, and he didn't want her to work, so that was kind of a conflict off and on.

Q: How large a family were you in?

Mr. Reagan: My sister Johnetta is a year younger than I. She's in Texas now. My brother William is nine years younger, and he had a career in the merchant service and retired. So there were three of us, and I was the oldest.

Q: What sort of work did your mother do?
_____
*His mother was Bernice Bonita Ector Reagan.

Mr. Reagan: My mother was a domestic most of the time.

Q: So you probably wound up looking after your brother and sister when she'd be out working.

Mr. Reagan: Yes, there was a lot of that. I was about nine years old when my brother was born. The family was together, and my mother was not working, because my dad had a pretty good job at Buick. In fact, he always did fairly well, average or better, because he worked that hard. We were poor but didn't know we were poor.

Q: Well, it was a relative thing. The country as a whole wasn't doing well.

Mr. Reagan: That's true. That's true. In Chicago, well, I guess I was just a bad little boy, running around with all the other kids. I don't remember anything too remarkable about it. The best memory I have of growing up is when we moved out to a neighborhood called Englewood, in Chicago.

Q: How old would you have been then?

Mr. Reagan: I'd say about 11, 12. As opposed to the East Side, where we'd lived before, the kids out in Englewood were more family oriented. They were interested in athletics, Boy Scouts, and that sort of thing. So I got a lot of positive motivation in that area. I started being a better than average athlete and a pretty good scholar, especially in playground activities, at first organized playground activities, and then in high school.

Q: Where had you gone to elementary school? Was that both in Flint and in Chicago?

Mr. Reagan: Yes. I don't remember too much about Flint. The biggest memory I have from there is that we had a pretty good-sized home, and we used to board some musicians. They would try to teach me how to play their various instruments. For a while, I thought I wasn't going to be anything but an entertainer. I don't remember too much about school in Flint.

Chicago is where I got most of my elementary education and high school. I went to Lindblom Technical High School. Mostly Eastern European kids. It was a large high school. There was Englewood High School, but Lindblom High School was where most of my friends attended, and I was right on the border, so I went to Lindblom.

Q: So these were integrated school situations?

Mr. Reagan: I think all of my education has been in an integrated environment, although Englewood, for example, became kind of a transitional area and mostly black, I would say.

Q: When did you first encounter prejudice or become aware of it?

Mr. Reagan: I think when I visited in Texas. I suppose I was 9, 10 years old, 11. I was always kind of big for my age, and some white kids pulled up in a car beside me once and used the word "nigger," and this sort of thing. That's, I think, the first time that I can recall feeling and perceiving that sort of thing.

Q: But it wasn't a day-by-day problem, I gather.

Mr. Reagan: No. I can say periodically I ran into it. When I first went to college up in Montana, the Chinese restaurant didn't want to serve me, and I happened to be going with some other football players, and there was no way they weren't going to serve me.* So we never had

---

*Mr. Reagan did his undergraduate study at Montana State University in Missoula. It is now named the University of Montana.

that problem anymore.

My school canceled Texas Tech off their schedule, because they said I would have to live with a family, not in the team hotel, when we returned the engagement. It seems that I was always in some sort of protective situation. I remember even once in the Navy, we went on the base in Norfolk, and the bus was really crowded. So I stepped up on the front, and the lady driver said, "You'll have to get off and go in the back."

"I can't get in the back."

So she said, "I'll just have to wait here for the cops."

I said, "I can't get back there. I want to get on this bus and go where I'm going."

Some kid, I guess he was from Wisconsin, got all mad and excited, saying, "Let the guy ride." So we had those kinds of experiences. I've had them periodically.

Even when I was an officer once down in Oxnard, California, we were getting ready to go overseas, nothing but sailors down there. I guess I was an ensign. I went into a restaurant, and the waiter did not want to seat me at a regular table. He said he would have to serve me in back, by the kitchen. I said, "No."

I finally called the base, so they sent an officer over, and he said, "You know, most of your business is with Navy people, and if you don't serve this gentleman, you're not going to serve anybody else. You're off-limits. Sorry."

Q: That's a very powerful persuader.

Mr. Reagan: Yes, the almighty dollar. Of course, when we went in the Navy, although the general service ratings were open, most of the things were segregated--Camp Robert Smalls.* We had a class A service school down at Hampton Roads, all black sailors. But then after we finished that, I don't think I encountered it in the Navy again.

Q: But it wasn't a real problem for you growing up in the North, I gather.

Mr. Reagan: I'd say, of course, because I lived in the North longer, that the instances I experienced were very far apart. I would class it an incident, where, for instance, an Irish guy went into an Italian neighborhood or something like that, which is racism in a sense.

Q: Wesley Brown said he was surprised when he got to the

---

*Within the Great Lakes Naval Training Station, Camp Robert Smalls was the site of training for black recruits during World War II. It was named for an escaped slave who captured the Confederate steamer Planter during the Civil War and turned her over to the U.S. Navy. He served as pilot of the Planter and later of the gunboat Keokuk.

J. W. Reagan #1 - 9

Naval Academy.* He felt the only kind of prejudice was against blacks, and he didn't know all these others existed.

Mr. Reagan: Well, I guess I learned about it a lot because of where I went to high school and things like that. I'd see how people treat each other.

Q: How early in life did you start setting some goals for what you'd like to become?

Mr. Reagan: I had a mother that, ever since I can remember, insisted that I could be anything I wanted to be. So, like most kids, I was a little bit impressionable. I got thinking that I'd like to be an entertainer, a musician. One time we lived with some people whose daughter Hazel was interested in dance. She married a black actor-comedian-entertainer named Mantan Moreland. She was in a group called the Blackbird Review, as I recall, and they would tour Europe and things like that. So she was teaching me how to dance and all this. So at one time, that's what I wanted to be. We moved away from them, and we've seen them occasionally on and off.

---

*Wesley A. Brown, Jr., class of 1949, was the first black graduate of the U.S. Naval Academy. He has been interviewed as part of the Naval Institute's oral history program.

J. W. Reagan #1 - 10

Then I got kind of serious about wanting to be a doctor. In fact, when I went to college, I took courses that would be leading to premed. I think the thing that stopped me there was that we had quantitative analysis or qualitative analysis or some chemistry course that interfered with football practice. So that wasn't the strongest goal in the world.

Q: Did you aspire to do anything in athletics, or was that an option at that point?

Mr. Reagan: I had a football scholarship. I had quite a successful time in athletics in high school. I had earned 12 or 13 letters--football, wrestling, boxing, track. I guess I would have played basketball, but they wouldn't let us do both football and basketball.

Q: Was that again for Lindblom?

Mr. Reagan: That was Lindblom. I won city and state championships in wrestling. Our whole backfield was supposed to go to the University of Michigan and did have offers from most of the Big Ten schools. But my wrestling coach, Mr. Spade, was a good friend of the football coach, Doug Fessenden, in Montana, and Spade talked me into going out there.*

---
*Douglas A. Fessenden was the head football coach at Montana State University from 1935 to 1941 and 1946 to 1948.

Q: You mentioned that you were a better than average student. What were some of the things you excelled in in high school?

Mr. Reagan: Well, when I say better than average, I mean I was always in the upper quarter of the class. I did well in English, because Mrs. Edwards was such an inspiration to me. She was an old lady with white hair, and she seemed to take a special interest in me.

Q: Graham Martin talked about the value of a teacher that is inspiring as well as informing.*

Mr. Reagan: Yes, and she wanted me to be a leader. This was her deal.

Q: Was your mother reinforcing that idea too?

Mr. Reagan: My mother was just 100% in back of me. Her deal was that if it's worth doing, it's worth doing well. She never tried to push me in any particular area, but she always supported me in whatever I was trying to do.

---
*Graham Edward Martin is a member of the Golden Thirteen. His oral history is in the Naval Institute collection.

Q: How big a factor was religion in your family when you were growing up?

Mr. Reagan: My father was spiritual, but he wasn't religious. However, in his later years, Dad became a staunch member and officer of his church in Marshall, Texas. My mother liked to go to church, sing in the choir, things like that.

I think I probably was a searcher. I was a Baptist, became a Catholic, went back to Baptist, became a Methodist--was always sort of searching. I think that I may, in a sense, be a lot like my father--that I consider myself pretty spiritual, but as far as dogmatic religion, I think that I'm not strongly in that sense. I have a very strong belief in God and try to treat other people like I'd like to be treated.

Q: Did your parents impart a sense of ethics and values to you?

Mr. Reagan: Oh, yes, very much so; both of them did. My father was very strong and very "moral" and very straight, inflexible. I think my mother was just the opposite, in that she had an outgoing, warm, and understanding personality.

J. W. Reagan #1 - 13

Q: Was she a shoulder to cry on if you needed one?

Mr. Reagan: Yes, I could always go to her about anything. They were quite different people, but they both, in their way, left some good things for me.

Q: Did you have time for other extracurricular activities besides all the sports you were in?

Mr. Reagan: I was secretary of the lettermen's club. I was the class chairman of the social committee, and I participated in Boy Scouts for quite a while.

Q: How high did you get in that hierarchy?

Mr. Reagan: I didn't get to be an Eagle Scout. I got far enough that we were participating in the big jamborees down at Soldier Field and all that sort of thing.* But it was a good influence on me. I met a fellow by the name of Arnett that was a good influence on my life at the time.

I had a good chance of going pretty sour, because a lot of the kids I knew and ran around with there later were involved with drugs--mostly marijuana--and crime and had very serious problems. I was lucky enough to escape that.

---
*Soldier Field is a large football stadium in downtown Chicago. Built in the 1920s, it is still in use as the home field of the Chicago Bears professional football team.

People like Arnett and some of the other people out in Englewood there became a pretty good influence for me.

Q: What was his capacity? Was he in the Scouts?

Mr. Reagan: Yes, he was a scoutmaster. He was a great gymnast, a health nut, and a moralist, in a sense. Not a preacher, but he was a guy that was always trying to lead you in the right direction. I'm not sure what Arnett's occupation was. I think he probably worked in the postal service. He was a great influence not only for me but a lot of kids in the neighborhood.

Q: Did you have jobs in your growing-up years?

Mr. Reagan: Oh, yes. I think I was working since I was 11 years old. My dad used to work for John F. Jelke Margarine Company in Chicago, and he washed those big trucks and did all the minor repairs and maintenance, such as tuneups, tire changing, lube, oil, and so forth. I used to go help him do that. Then, whenever he had time otherwise, we would go around polishing cars for some of the officers in the company and others.

At 15, I lied about my age and got a job in a steel foundry, chipping tractor axles. That involved working with a partner to pick up the axles after they came from the foundry and setting them on a type of conveyor. We walked along chipping the excess metal off before they went on to other finishing procedures.

I also had one year on a farm. I don't remember not working, ever.

Q: Was the steel foundry over in Gary, Indiana?

Mr. Reagan: No, it was in Chicago. This was National Malleable and Steel Company.

Q: Did you have a chance to form a bond with your father, going camping or to ball games and that sort of thing?

Mr. Reagan: I think the most I got with Dad, except at the end, was when we were working together. That was quite a bit, because he worked, like I said, two or three jobs. We had a nice house. I especially remember that since I got in real estate. I think we had a three- or four-bedroom, two-story house, and the rent was something like $25.00 a month. So when he would make $100.00 or $150.00 a month, we did pretty well in those days. I look back at that and say, "If you could get by in a week on that now, you'd really be doing something."

Q: How much did you develop an interest in reading,

J. W. Reagan #1 - 16

keeping up with the outside world?

Mr. Reagan: A lot. When I was very small, I was in the library a lot, and I was always looking at things beyond my comprehension, even astrology and stuff like that. I was a great dreamer. Then somehow I got out of it, because I got the perception that it wasn't good to be dreaming all the time.

Q: Well, it's normal for kids.

Mr. Reagan: I know, but I was fascinated with books and pictures and things like that. I've liked to look at them ever since I can remember. So I don't read a lot of books now, but I do a lot of reading. I like to read about current events. I like to look at financial stuff and things like that.

Q: Was the radio popular in your household when you were growing up?

Mr. Reagan: Oh, yes. I remember the earphones and all that, listening to the Hoover-Roosevelt campaign and "Amos and Andy."*

---
*Franklin D. Roosevelt defeated Herbert C. Hoover in the 1932 presidential election. "Amos and Andy" was a radio comedy program in which two white actors portrayed black men.

Q: What was the perception in the black community of the "Amos and Andy" show?

Mr. Reagan: We used to laugh like hell at it, I know, in the family. It was a lot of years later, when the "black is beautiful" era started coming along, then there were criticisms about "Amos and Andy."

Q: Retroactively.

Mr. Reagan: Retroactively, yes. But we wouldn't miss it. In fact, that's about the biggest show I remember that we had fun with in those years, in Flint, Michigan, mostly.

Q: How much did you keep track of the European situation? It was growing steadily worse in the Thirties.

Mr. Reagan: I believe I was just aware of it. During the Thirties, I was still in my teens. I was aware of Communism and all this sort of thing, and that's another thing that I was very lucky to somehow miss. I don't know how I missed getting involved with them, because some of them used to come over in the neighborhood and invite the fellows to the picnics where there were going to be food, girls, music, and all. I don't know how I never got involved with it, but some of the fellows did.

Q: Paul Robeson is a very famous example.*

Mr. Reagan: That's right. I won't forget Paul, because when we were playing Gonzaga University in Butte, Montana, for some reason Paul Robeson was there. He was still very popular. I, in fact, shook his hand and spoke very briefly with him at that time, because I had a good game, and he was a great athlete. But, of course, I remember the so-called McCarthy era and things of that type.** I was aware of things that were going on, and, I guess, also quite busy with my own activities.

Q: At that time, nobody really knew how evil Hitler was.***

Mr. Reagan: That's right.

Q: A lot of that came out later.

---
*Paul Robeson (1898-1967) was a distinguished black singer, actor, and athlete. He ran afoul of the U.S. Government because of his interest in Russia and Communism.
**In the early 1950s, Senator Joseph R. McCarthy (Republican from Wisconsin) conducted a series of congressional investigations aimed at uncovering the presence of Communists in the U.S. Government and various industries.
***Adolf Hitler was Chancellor of Germany, 1933-45.

J. W. Reagan #1 - 19

Mr. Reagan: See, I finished high school in '39. I started college in the fall of that year.

Q: That was just as the war was starting in Europe.

Mr. Reagan: Yes. In 1940, the Army Air Corps recruiting team came around to the campus and tried to sign me up. I didn't see any war or anything then, although things were going on over there. But I was interested in my football and my education and this sort of thing, so I didn't sign up. In 1941, after Pearl Harbor, they came around again, and I did sign up. In fact, the summer before, I had registered for the draft, too, but I didn't want to be drafted. So I signed up for the Air Force.*

Later, of course, I joined the Navy, and a week after I was out at Great Lakes, in boot camp, I got orders to go down to Tuskegee, where they were training the 99th Pursuit Squadron.** I went up to the executive officer and said, "I've only been in the Navy a week, and I've got these orders where I can be a flier. Can't you let me out?"

He said, "No way. We'll have black pilots in the Navy

---
*In June 1941, the name of the service was officially changed from U.S. Army Air Corps to U.S. Army Air Forces. In 1947, it became a separate service, namely, U.S. Air Force.
**The Army Air Forces established a training program for black pilots at Tuskegee, Alabama, site of the Tuskegee Institute.

J. W. Reagan #1 - 20

some day." So I was pretty unhappy about that.

Q: Why did you go ahead and join the Navy after you were already in the Army Air Forces?

Mr. Reagan: At the end of the winter quarter, I know I had signed up for the Air Force; I know I had passed whatever selection procedures they had. I went home, back to Chicago, with my dad. My mother was living in California at the time. I said, "Well, there's no need of my going back to school, because the Air Force is going to call me." When I didn't go back to school, the draft board got very interested in me, too, so I worked in the stockyards for a while, and then the draft board said, "We can't hold off much longer. We have to take you."

So I said, "No, I don't want to be drafted."

Q: So you didn't actually enlist in the Air Force? Was it more of a tentative type thing?

Mr. Reagan: I didn't get the orders until after I had enlisted in the Navy.

Q: I see.

Mr. Reagan: It was in November or December of 1941 that

J. W. Reagan #1 - 21

the Air Force recruiting people came around to the campus. When I went home that winter, I kept saying, "I'm expecting to go in the Air Force," and I thought it would be in three months. In fact, it was July before I enlisted in the Navy.

Q: So the Air Force sort of said, "Don't call us, we'll call you when we're ready to take you."

Mr. Reagan: Yes. I don't know why it took so long, but anyway, I finally did get orders, but I was in the Navy.

Q: So how many years did you spend at Montana State?

Mr. Reagan: I started school in '39, but I couldn't play football as a freshman. I played in my sophomore year.

Q: Okay, that would be in the fall of '40.

Mr. Reagan: Yes. Then, at the end of '41, I left school. Then in July of '42, I enlisted in the Navy.

Q: You had maybe about five semesters at Montana State?

Mr. Reagan: Yes, at that time. Then, after the war, I came back. See, I calculate that I finished my college in about three and a half years.

Q: What sort of grades were you making when you were there?

Mr. Reagan: I made very good grades, except in chemistry. I just got by in chemistry. But I think I switched because it was more compatible with football, and I took economics and sociology, and my grades were very good. In my whole college scholastic career, I was a scholar-athlete. I don't know where I finished in the class, but it was good enough to get that designation.

Q: How good a football player were you? Don't be modest.

Mr. Reagan: I was pretty good. We were in the Pacific Coast Conference--Montana, Idaho, UCLA, and we played the Washington and Oregon schools. We only had a token schedule each year and were never quite a serious choice to win the coast conference. Theoretically, we had a shot at the Rose Bowl. We beat everybody except the large schools. We just didn't have the staying power. I made all-American honorable mention at the end of my first year of varsity ball.

Then after the war, when I came back and finished my last year of eligibility, I made some all-coast designation. Then I played pro ball in Canada. I was a pretty fair football player.

Q: What position did you play?

Mr. Reagan: I was a back. The coach had me playing quarterback for a while; this is after I came back. I was a blocking back prior to that.

Q: Was this in the single wing?

Mr. Reagan: Yes, single wing, double wing, box formation. So I was a fullback, blocking back type. Then after the war, the coach came back and tried to make a T-formation quarterback out of me. I could pass, but running and blocking were my fortes. I think I played one semester. Then I went on up to Canada. They had five backs, and I was the guy in back of all of them. I generally handled the ball on every play, either run or pass.

Q: How fast were you?

Mr. Reagan: Probably not better than ten.* I wouldn't say that I was a speed-burner like the guys are today.

_____
*This is a reference to a time of 10.0 seconds for the 100-yard dash.

J. W. Reagan #1 - 24

Q: Well, ten is not shabby.

Mr. Reagan: I think that would probably be my best in the 100.

Q: Dr. Barnes, for example, was a sprinter.*

Mr. Reagan: Yes, Barnes was a good athlete.

Q: I've been struck--that is the one common thread that I've observed among the Golden Thirteen, that so many of you were good athletes.

Mr. Reagan: Yes, a lot of the guys. I think Sublett went to the University of Wisconsin. Jesse Arbor . . .**

Q: Dalton Baugh.***

Mr. Reagan: Dalton Baugh, right. Yes, that's true. You asked me about goals. Of course, we're getting up into the Navy situation now. I had some ROTC in college, and when we went into the Navy and went to boot camp as apprentice

---

*Samuel Edward Barnes is a member of the Golden Thirteen. His oral history is in the Naval Institute collection.
**Jesse Walter Arbor is a member of the Golden Thirteen. His oral history is in the Naval Institute collection.
***Dalton Louis Baugh was a member of the Golden Thirteen. He died before he could be interviewed for an oral history.

seamen, it seems like some of us were just selected to be the ACPOs of the company, and sometimes some of us ran the company.* The chief would come around and watch us to see how we handled things.

Q: Had you enlisted in Chicago?

Mr. Reagan: Yes.

Q: The Navy at that point looked more desirable than getting drafted, I take it.

Mr. Reagan: I had a philosophical difficulty with having to go in by being drafted. The kids that I was in school with, mostly white youngsters--I knew some of them were officers in ROTC, and I knew these guys were going out in all sorts of things, doing great jobs and all that. I wanted to do one too. I didn't want to feel that I had to go in the service because somebody was drafting me. The night of Pearl Harbor, I think I was in a movie in Montana, and there were extras on the street after we got out of the movie. I was determined to go in the service then, but I didn't want to be drafted.

---

*ROTC--reserve officer training corps; ACPOs--apprentice chief petty officers.

Q: Why then did you settle on the Navy?

Mr. Reagan: I think the idea of eventually being able to go aboard ship and traveling maybe just felt better to me. At the time, we knew that the general service ratings were open.* So it was more appealing to me—other than the Air Force. I really wanted to go in the Air Force.

Q: Was the proximity of training at Great Lakes a factor at all?

Mr. Reagan: No. I wanted to get away from Chicago. I really wanted to travel.

Q: You didn't have any girlfriends tying you down?

Mr. Reagan: Oh, I had girlfriends, yes. But I still wanted to get away. In fact, maybe that's why I wanted to get away; I had more than one. I met my first wife in Hampton at class A service school.

Q: What do you remember about your initial indoctrination at Camp Robert Smalls?

---

*Effective in June 1942, the Navy began enlisting blacks for entry into the general service ratings rather than just as cooks and stewards.

Mr. Reagan: I remember I had this attitude that, "I'm going to be the best sailor I can be, and I want this company to be the best outfit it can be, and I want every black guy in the Navy to be the best he can be." I wouldn't call it gung-ho; it's just the way I felt. Because the Navy hadn't had us in general services ratings in recent history, anyway. So I suppose this attitude kind of came out, and that may be why I was chosen as apprentice chief petty officer of the company.

Later, when we went to service school, Sublett was the battalion commander, and I was the adjutant. I don't remember pushing for these things, necessarily. The most surprising thing in my life was when I had to go to Great Lakes for this officers' class, and I was very unhappy about it, because I'd gone through class A electrical school, and I was an electrician's mate, and I had been ordered to go from Point Loma out here. I was on an auxiliary minesweep, and I had been ordered to Norfolk to go aboard a DE as an AC electrician.* Boy, I was a petty officer second class, and that was really something.

Commander Downes, who was the skipper of the training school at Hampton, just happened to be over at Norfolk on the base, and he saw me and said, "What the hell are you

_____
*DE--destroyer escort; AC--alternating current.

J. W. Reagan #1 - 28

doing over here?"*

I was so proud. I said, "Skipper, I'm going aboard this DE as an AC electrician's mate. I'm going to get a ship at last."

He said, "The hell you are! Come over here to the personnel office and get your orders changed. You come over to my quarters at the school this afternoon or this evening, and I'll tell you a little bit about what's going on."

So I did, and he didn't tell me, actually, that it was an officers' indoctrination. He said, "We're sending you up to Great Lakes for a special class, and it's something that you'll like. You'll be glad you're going. It might lead to something that you never suspected." Sort of that tone of things. Then we talked a little bit about what I'd been doing in the Navy and things like that.

Q: Had he known you before, from your service school time?

Mr. Reagan: Oh, yes, because Sublett and I ran the battalion previously when we were students there.

Q: But he worked through you.

---
*Lieutenant Commander Edwin H. Downes, USNR, was officer in charge of the Naval Training School, Hampton, Virginia. He had been graduated from the Naval Academy in the class of 1920, resigned as an ensign in 1922, and earned a master's degree in education. In 1941, he was recalled to active duty as a Naval Reserve officer.

Mr. Reagan: Yes, and through, of course, the other officers on his staff, but he knew us well. He knew everybody. In fact, I think he could call everybody in that battalion by name. They had the electrical school, the diesel school, the machinist's mate school; I think those were the main schools that they had down there.

Q: Great Lakes and the service school at Hampton seem to be the two main sources for your group of officer candidates.

Mr. Reagan: Yes, yes. When they decided to make black officers, there was supposed to be some large, large number of people that they screened down to those 13. I think that the commanding officers' recommendations where you'd served before were pretty important at the time, as I understand it. I think that's why he was upset when he saw me at Norfolk, because I think the rest of the guys were up at Great Lakes already. I guess nobody could find me yet.

Q: Baugh came out of that group, too, didn't he?

Mr. Reagan: Yes, he did. Baugh was at Hampton; Sublett too. Baugh, Sublett, Cooper.

Q: Cooper was an instructor there.*

Mr. Reagan: Cooper was an instructor, right. Gravely was there, too, I think.**

Q: Yes. Did you ever find out, then or later, why you happened to be included in that group?

Mr. Reagan: Only from Downes. I know that Downes had recommended me. That's really the only thing I know. I did well in service school, I did pretty well on the base. We graduated from Hampton as third class petty officers, and as soon as it was time to take the second class, I took the second class. Of course, when they made us officer candidates, they made us first class.

Q: What do you remember about your leadership responsibilities, both at boot camp and in the service school? For example, were you calling the cadence when units would march?

Mr. Reagan: Sublett and I would exchange doing that, yes.

---

*George Clinton Cooper was a member of the Golden Thirteen. His oral history is in the Naval Institute collection.
**Samuel L. Gravely, Jr., was an enlisted man at that time. In the early 1970s, he became the first black flag officer in the U.S. Navy. His oral history is in the Naval Institute collection.

J. W. Reagan #1 - 31

You know, I was the adjutant, so he'd give me orders, and I'd about-face and give them to the battalion. Yes, we did that, and we also kept the barracks in shape. We had kind of a shipshape outfit.

Q: You talked about this motivation to excel. I would think that patriotism was part of that also.

Mr. Reagan: There's no question about it. There was never any question in my mind about my wanting to serve the country. I felt, and still do, that fighting for the country was a part of fighting for equality.

Q: How soon did you find out that you actually were to be trained to become a commissioned officer?

Mr. Reagan: When I got to Great Lakes, the other guys already knew. I said, "What the hell's this all about? I'm just ready to go on a ship, you know."

"We're going to have an officers' class." I don't think I knew until then. I've heard several other guys say that they weren't sure what was going on, and I don't know if we believed it even then. They had this class. We had a whole barracks to ourselves for this class of 16.

Q: Was it a large barracks intended for many more?

J. W. Reagan #1 - 32

Mr. Reagan: Yes, it was like a company barracks. We had the run of it.

Q: Was it divided into individual rooms, or was it a large, open bay?

Mr. Reagan: Yes, I think it was open. We had slept in hammocks earlier when I was in boot training. In these barracks we had bunks. I recall doing the sheets and hanging them up on the tile wall in the head to dry out, so it would look like they were ironed.

Q: Did you have any contact with Commander Armstrong?*

Mr. Reagan: Very little. Dennis seemed to have had a lot with him.** I knew him and had probably been in his company.

Q: I gather that Goodwin was pretty much the go-between to Armstrong.***

---

*Commander Daniel W. Armstrong, USNR, was officer in charge of Camp Robert Smalls. A 1915 graduate of the Naval Academy, he resigned his regular commission in 1919 to pursue a civilian career, then was recalled to active duty as a reserve officer in World War II.
**Dennis Denmark Nelson II was a member of the Golden Thirteen. He died before he could be interviewed by the Naval Institute's oral history program.
***Reginald Ernest Goodwin was a member of the Golden Thirteen. He died before he could be interviewed by the Naval Institute's oral history program.

J. W. Reagan #1 - 33

Mr. Reagan: Yes, Goodwin was. Dennis had some negative feelings about Armstrong.

Q: Based on what? Do you have any knowledge?

Mr. Reagan: I think one of the first things that came out when we were becoming officers was that we were not supposed to go in the officers' club on the main side, things like that. I never did know specifically what it was with Dennis. I read Dennis's book, and I've heard him talk in a negative fashion, but I tended to let it go in one ear and out of the other, because I was not directly involved, so I didn't quite understand what was going on.* But I didn't have any direct contact with him, enough, in fact, for me to have any particular feelings about him one way or the other. He was a fine-looking officer.

Q: What was the attitude of the instructors during your officer training? Were they in any sense condescending?

Mr. Reagan: I don't think so. I think our instructors were great. I think they were dedicated to doing a good job with us.

---

*Dennis D. Nelson, The Integration of the Negro into the U.S. Navy (New York: Farrar, Strauss and Young, 1951).

Q: What are the professional subjects you recall that they covered?

Mr. Reagan: Well, Navy regs, of course, navigation, communications. I don't know if we had some personnel administration. Naval history. Of course, we had the gunnery classes and things like that.

Q: How did the pace and difficulty of instruction compare with what you had at college in Montana?

Mr. Reagan: I didn't have any problem with it. I don't know why, but I just don't recall having any big problem with it. I know that some of the guys studied all night. I may have done it once in a while. I don't recall having any great deal of pressure in that class about the studies.

Q: One thing I've been struck by, and the others have told me, that there was a consensus to cooperate rather than compete.

Mr. Reagan: No question about that. No question about it. I mean, if somebody didn't know something, he'd better ask. It was absolutely great, the way everybody worked together, stuck together, and supported each other.

Q: Was there any aspect of the training devoted to the way that an officer and gentleman behaves compared with enlisted?

Mr. Reagan: Oh, yes. Oh, sure.

Q: Any specifics you remember in that regard?

Mr. Reagan: I don't recall any, because by that time, we'd mostly been in the Navy for a while. It wouldn't strike me as being something unusual, because we already knew a lot of that indoctrinational type stuff anyway, about relationships between officers and enlisted people, and things like that. I don't recall anything outstanding about that part of the training.

Q: Was there any discussion of the possibility that you might face difficulties that white officers didn't?

Mr. Reagan: I would say that I don't think that was emphasized. I think there was a general sense about it, and I think in a way that's what it was almost all about.

Q: Just your experience as a human being, you knew that there would be problems.

Mr. Reagan: Right. We knew, I guess, generally, the southern tradition in the Navy. I think we knew all of this, but in our minds, individually and collectively, this wasn't going to stop us from doing the best job possible.

Q: Did you have a sense at the time you were undergoing the training what a historic step it was? Did you have a chance to reflect on it?

Mr. Reagan: We were very much aware of it. It was a part of everybody's motivation to do well, because I think we had a sense that what we did may affect what other people had a chance to do.

Q: Collective failure could have been very costly.

Mr. Reagan: That's right, I'm sure. I'll tell you, the high-ranking fellows now, the high-ranking black officers now, the young guys, they honor us. They show us a great deal of respect and say, "If it hadn't been for you guys, we wouldn't be here"--admirals on down. They don't know how awestruck I am about them. Gravely's been a commander of a fleet, and others have commanded ships and aircraft squadrons. You know, this is something that's just tremendous. When they come and say, "If it hadn't been for

J. W. Reagan #1 - 37

you guys," I say, "What the hell did we do? You guys are where it's at."

Q: Each person has his own destiny to fulfill.

Mr. Reagan: Yes. I'm very proud of the young fellows.

Q: How would you describe a typical day during that officer training period?

Mr. Reagan: I don't recall the exact day. I know we had exercise, we had breakfast, and then classes right away. So, I guess, we would have about two or three classes during the course of the day, depending on what the subject was, and knock off at 5:00-6:00 o'clock, when everybody else knocked off for chow. The evenings, we studied.

Q: Was there a fair amount of drilling and marching?

Mr. Reagan: Not too much of that at that time. I think we marched to chow as a group.

Q: Did you feel uncomfortable in being isolated from everybody else?

Mr. Reagan: It was noticed, but I don't recall feeling too

uncomfortable about it. I thought that that particular setting was possibly the best setting available for what they were trying to do with us.

Q: It got rid of distractions.

Mr. Reagan: Yes. I accepted it for that, anyway.

Q: I gather there wasn't much of an opportunity for liberty either.

Mr. Reagan: Only on weekends, as I recall. Weekends.

Q: Did you get to visit your family during that time?

Mr. Reagan: Yes, and some of the guys were married too.

Q: One thing I've learned is that each man contributed in a special area of expertise that he added to the collective group knowledge. What things were you particularly strong in?

Mr. Reagan: Yes. Of course, I was an electrician's mate, and I guess some technical things that would come up, I had a pretty good perception of. I would say that maybe I was more of a generalist in the group.

Q: You and Sublett, as the youngest, did you tend to take your guidance from some of the others more?

Mr. Reagan: I don't think so. I mean, I'm not saying that in any disrespectful way, but I just don't recall that we felt any different about any of the guys because they were a little older.

Q: Were there any specific leaders in the group?

Mr. Reagan: I'd say that I think, in a sense, all the guys were, but it wasn't a situation of conflict. Maybe there were differences about something, but there was always consensus, and there was always discussion.

Q: Are there any specific incidents that stand out in your mind from that training period? Any particular highlights?

Mr. Reagan: Well, I think I tend to remember the day of the final examinations, and then after training we were individually notified. I guess the orders were cut, or however they did it, and this tended to create some anxiety and tension. The guys that hadn't been informed were wondering whether they were going to make it or not.

Q: Did you feel a sadness that three of your group did not make it through?

Mr. Reagan: Oh, yes.

Q: Did you have any knowledge of why those three didn't? The three were Alves, Pinkney, and Williams.*

Mr. Reagan: I heard a rumor that Alves had passed for Portuguese or something at one time. He was light-skinned, straight hair, and I guess he could have. That was a rumor. Williams--it seemed to me there was something about his education that he had indicated that wasn't so. I guess they had a hell of a background check on us.

Q: Those things sound like things that would have turned up, though, before people were put in the group.

Mr. Reagan: Yes, you'd think so, you know, because it was supposed to be quite a screening job done on us.

Q: How much were you aware of the investigation into your own background?

Mr. Reagan: Not much at all. I don't recall anybody

---
*A. Alves, J. B. Pinkney, and Lewis R. Williams.

J. W. Reagan #1 - 41

telling me that somebody was coming around asking questions about me or anything.

Q: George Cooper said they were so thorough in his case that they knew about a fistfight he'd gotten into when he was eight years old.

Mr. Reagan: Well, if I'd gotten involved with that Communist Party when I was a kid, I would have really had a problem, wouldn't I? I don't recall any knowledge. In fact, I just didn't know anything until I got up to Great Lakes, except for what Commander Downes said.

Q: I have read one assertion that the Navy arbitrarily decided that only 13 of the group were going to pass.*

Mr. Reagan: It could have been that it was more of an exclusionary procedure, I guess.

Q: Were your grades posted so you could be compared with each other?

---
*Bernard C. Nalty, Strength for the Fight (New York: The Free Press, 1986), makes the following statement on page 192: " . . . on January 1, 1944, sixteen black enlisted men entered a segregated officer candidate school at the Great Lakes Naval Training Station. Although all of them successfully completed the course, only twelve received commissions, a purely arbitrary number adopted by the Bureau of Personnel for reasons never explained. Of the remaining four, one became a warrant officer, and the others reverted to enlisted status."

Mr. Reagan: I don't recall that that was done. It could have been, but I don't recall it.

Q: Were you aware of your own marks individually? Were you given that?

Mr. Reagan: I'm pretty sure we were, because we had frequent tests. I don't recall any great worry about any of the classes that we had. If there was a book on it and there was something to read about it, I could always pass the test. I don't mean I'd know everything, but I could pass tests. So I never remember having great concern about any of those classes. But we did study and did our assignments and all of that.

Q: Would you describe yourself as a quick study, with an ability to absorb material quickly?

Mr. Reagan: I would say yes. However, I'll tell you one thing. I feel that sometimes you come across something that you don't understand right off the bat, and you have to struggle a little bit for. I think I learned a lot more that way.

Q: Were the instructors helpful in explaining things that you might not understand?

Mr. Reagan: Oh, yes.

Q: Are there any instructors you remember individually?

Mr. Reagan: I remember Chief Payton.* I remember him more for his manner and his manner of presentation, more than the content of what he was talking about.

Q: What was so striking about his manner?

Mr. Reagan: He was very articulate. He was a black man. I think he had been an instructor at Hampton. He was just very articulate and suave and, you know, I was just impressed with him generally.

Q: I'd just like to run through the names of the individuals in your group, and get your memories, thumbnail sketches, perhaps.

Mr. Reagan: Okay.

Q: Jesse Arbor.

---
*Chief Petty Officer Noble Payton.

Mr. Reagan: I love Arbor. Arbor always has a story, and though he's always outgoing, he's always got a story and a lot of humor to him. But I think he's a pretty deep guy, really, behind all of it, a very good thinker, a lot of common sense. With his size and everything, he's just an unforgettable character.

Q: I got the impression he was something of a cheerleader in the group to bring the morale up.

Mr. Reagan: Yes, always.

Q: And just such a good-hearted soul, willing to give of himself.

Mr. Reagan: No question about it. He does. Jesse's just the kind of guy that if you were having a crisis of some kind, you'd like for him to be there.

Q: Maybe a wisecrack to dispel the tension.

Mr. Reagan: Yes, yes. He and Dennis Nelson had more stories than anybody I know, I think, in any walk of life.

Q: Were they joke-type stories or anecdotes or what?

Mr. Reagan: Anecdotes, yes, and almost anything you'd bring up, he'd have a humorous story or incident or event. Sometimes they were told as the gospel truth, and you know they're not. It just amazes me how anyone can constantly come up with those sort of things.

Q: Phillip Barnes.*

Mr. Reagan: Phil I didn't know too well, but Phil impressed me as a very serious person. He was all business. I didn't have a really close relationship with him, other than in the class.

Q: He had a sister who was able to get you some information from Washington, I gather.

Mr. Reagan: That's what I understand. I don't recall having known that personally, but I understand that that was maybe how guys knew things before it was official.

Q: Samuel Barnes.

Mr. Reagan: Love Sam. Sam was--how can I describe Sam?

---
*Phillip George Barnes was a member of the Golden Thirteen. He died before he could be interviewed as part of the Naval Institute's oral history program.

Q: In many ways, he's the opposite of Arbor.

Mr. Reagan: Yes, he is, but he has a good sense of humor, too, but it's more a wry type. I would say Sam was a sort of a father confessor type, I think. If I had problems, I think I'd like to talk to Sam about them.

Q: Do you remember any specific incidents?

Mr. Reagan: Not really, but I personally just felt very comfortable around Sam and felt that he was a guy that had a lot of understanding about life, in general, and just kind of a nice guy to be around.

Q: Dalton Baugh.

Mr. Reagan: Dalton and I were good buddies for one period there, as we were together a lot. I think it was primarily there in Chicago and throughout, periodically, to the end. Dalton had, in my estimation, a brilliant mind, but he was a "good old boy" type, as far as our relationship went, and, I suppose, with everybody else. He had a tremendous personality.

Q: You would describe him as outgoing also?

Mr. Reagan: Yes, I would have to--not perhaps as much as Dennis or as much as Jesse. A little more serious, but definitely not a wallflower. He was aggressive in a quiet sort of way. Naturally, he would have to, to start a business and things like that, and work it through. I recall visiting him when he was at MIT, doing research there.* Just a good, solid guy, very smart, a lot of common sense. A lot of those fellows from Arkansas had good old down-to-earth common sense, took the time to think through a situation.

Q: I think the Navy picked well in assembling this group. In that sense, it was a good-faith effort.

Mr. Reagan: Yes, I think you realize that, when you look back on it, and you think about the group. I think we know it more since we've gotten together than we probably recognized at that time.

Q: George Cooper.

Mr. Reagan: How would I describe George? George is pretty much all business too. George, I think, probably exhibited as much or more maturity in the group than anyone that I

___
*MIT--Massachusetts Institute of Technology, Cambridge, Massachusetts.

can think of.

Q: How was that manifested?

Mr. Reagan: I think mostly in his analysis of situations, in his demeanor and personality.

Q: He's a very dignified person.

Mr. Reagan: Very dignified, and very smart too.

Q: I've been struck by his ability to plan and organize situations.

Mr. Reagan: He is an organizer. He is an organizer. I guess that's a good way to say it. I think it shows a lot in his civilian career, director of community development there at Dayton.

Q: He's got a new enterprise going now, to set up a day care center and subcontractor for an auto plant.

Mr. Reagan: It doesn't surprise me. He had some interest in Africa at one time. I imagine it's hard for most of the guys to actually retire. I'm as busy as I ever was. But I

J. W. Reagan #1 - 49

don't think it's a retiring type of group of individuals. I don't know what Jim Hair is doing now, but I know he's active in community activities.*

Q: What do you remember about Reginald Goodwin?

Mr. Reagan: Not too much. I didn't know Goodwin too well. Goodwin was another guy that, I think, was pretty much all business too. I don't know. Goodwin might have been the disciplinarian in the group. He just might have been.

Q: I think he probably had been in the Navy longer than some of the others, hadn't he?

Mr. Reagan: Yes, he had.

Q: Soaked up some of that Navy tradition.

Mr. Reagan: Right. Like you say, I think he had kind of a close tie with Armstrong. But he was, as I recall, a serious individual and wanted to make sure that we all toed the line.

Q: James Hair.

---
*James Edward Hair is a member of the Golden Thirteen. His oral history is in the Naval Institute collection.

Mr. Reagan: Jim Hair and I spent a lot of time together in New York. Jim was the skipper of a tugboat, and I was aboard that with him. We spent a lot of time together socially. Jim is just a great all-around individual. I think he has all the good qualities of all the guys in the group, a very good officer and ship handler.

Q: A very sunny disposition.

Mr. Reagan: A beautiful disposition, just beautiful. But if a situation requires him to be very stern and strict-- and I think all of the guys had that quality, too, but his predominant disposition and personality was one of calm deliberation, timely action, and a nice sense of humor.

Q: Interestingly, he had been exposed to the negative aspects of the race situation perhaps more than any of you, growing up in the South, losing a brother-in-law to a lynching.

Mr. Reagan: Yes. There's nothing in my experience that has been that tough. A few insults or something occasionally, but nothing that tragic.

Q: Is that the sort of thing he ever talked about? Did

J. W. Reagan #1 - 51

you share backgrounds?

Mr. Reagan: No. Well, Jim talked. Jim was a great family guy. He had about 13 brothers and sisters, something like that. He would occasionally talk about his brothers and sisters, but as much time as we spent together, we never really went into background in any great depth.

Q: Was there much chance during that training period to just shoot the breeze in off-duty type situations?

Mr. Reagan: Oh, yes. Most of the guys could lie real well. Most of them had stories to tell. I recall, not on a specific subject, but shooting the breeze about the day, about the subjects, and about things of this type. The guys teased each other about personal things that they knew. There were little groupings, a subgroup of guys that had known each other and gone on liberty together and things like that, so they played around with each other and kidded each other about things.

Q: Charles Lear.

Mr. Reagan: Charlie loved the Navy. He loved the Navy. As I recall, he was so happy to be included in that group, and I just think he was a Navy guy through and through.

J. W. Reagan #1 - 52

That's the biggest impression I have about Charles. I heard about this unfortunate tragedy, about his great desire to become regular Navy.*

Q: Not being able to was what so disappointed him.

Mr. Reagan: Yes. He was really, really gung-ho about the Navy, and I can understand that. I think we all were, but my impression was that the Navy was all there was for Charles. He did not consider other options, in my opinion.

Q: Weren't he and Nelson the two that were strongest in that regard?

Mr. Reagan: Yes, yes, they were. Of course, I spent a lot more time with Dennis than I did with Lear. I knew Dennis a lot better. They were very similar in their desire to be a part of the Navy.

Q: What was Lear like during the training period?

Mr. Reagan: I think Lear was pretty serious. I don't recall anything outstanding about him in terms of personality, except that he was serious, and I think he was

---

*Charles Byrd Lear was a member of the Golden Thirteen. He committed suicide following his release from active naval service after World War II.

J. W. Reagan #1 - 53

probably the seamanship guy in the group. Just a kind of serious and very nice man, a nice, nice person generally.

Q: Considerate of others.

Mr. Reagan: Yes, yes. He's another guy that you could feel comfortable being around; you could talk or not talk, or whatever.

Q: Were there any in the group that you would say you didn't feel comfortable around?

Mr. Reagan: I can't say that, no.

Q: What are your recollections of Graham Martin?*

Mr. Reagan: Of course, Graham was a fine athlete too. We had a lot of rapport there.

Q: Did the athletes have a subgroup of their own?

Mr. Reagan: Not really. I just knew that he had been a star player on the Great Lakes team. I think Graham is a strongly religious person, and he's strong, period, as we know now, if we didn't know then. He and his wife Alma

___
*Graham Edward Martin is a member of the Golden Thirteen. His oral history is in the Naval Institute collection.

deal with each other's problems in an inspiring way.

Q: His devotion to his wife is just remarkable.

Mr. Reagan: It's outstanding. They don't want you to do anything for them. Graham says, "Get out of the way. I'll do this." Or help her in her wheelchair, things like that. Alma says, "Let Graham do that." They're beautiful people.

Q: I'd say another common denominator of the group is great pride.

Mr. Reagan: I think so, yes. Oh, yes.

Q: Perhaps none more so than Dennis Nelson.

Mr. Reagan: Oh, Dennis was the epitome of pride. I don't know if this is a figment of my imagination or not, but it really seems to me that the first uniform Dennis bought was a formal one and a sword. We were all trying to get grays and khakis. Dennis got downtown, I believe, and he had the cape. He had everything from the start, you know. He always had a nice car--outside, engine, clean off the engine. No matter where he was, he would get up and wash his car every morning, even if it was in a garage, and

J. W. Reagan #1 - 55

generally it was.

Q: A great fetish for cleanliness.

Mr. Reagan: Cleanliness and substance too. He put himself on the line. Dennis is the cause of my spending eight years in the Navy, total. After the war, following up on this equal opportunity thing, he brought some black officers and petty officers back on active duty. I don't know who else came back besides myself. I think that was his plan, to get these people back on active duty and have them traveling all around, first on the East Coast, trying to get people interested in the NROTC programs.

While I was in, the Korean War came up, so I had another four-year tour. I was just looking at my DD 214 the other day, and I had almost 12 years of service for pay purposes.* I think I was probably in for 23 years total, including reserve time. But somewhere along age 40 I thought I was too busy to keep going on the two-week tours and keep up the correspondence courses. Back then I didn't think I'd live to be 60. I'd be drawing a pretty big check now, because I did make lieutenant commander in the reserves.

Q: But you didn't qualify for retirement?

---
*DD 214 is a Department of Defense form issued to individuals leaving active duty.

J. W. Reagan #1 - 56

Mr. Reagan: No. It seems to me I had about 18 years of good time.

Q: That's close. Too bad you didn't get the other two.

Mr. Reagan: Yes, I can see that now.

Q: What do you remember about Frank Sublett?

Mr. Reagan: Great buddy. Great buddy. I think we could be brothers, because we're a lot alike. Probably a lot in the background, and I think we think a lot alike. Of course, people believe in that stuff. We're both Pisces, same day, same month, same year.

Q: That's a remarkable coincidence for that small a group.

Mr. Reagan: Yes. Sublett was great. He was great militarily, had a great, booming voice, and kind of quiet, but when he speaks, you hear him.

Q: Syl White.*

---
*William Sylvester White is a member of the Golden Thirteen. His oral history is in the Naval Institute collection.

Mr. Reagan: Syl. Syl is judicial, as you know. I think that's his personality. He's a judge.

Q: Did you see aspects of it in the training period?

Mr. Reagan: I think so. He was quiet and meditative.

Q: Would you sort of compare him with George Cooper in that respect?

Mr. Reagan: I have to think about that. I'm not impressed that they were a lot alike.

Q: They're both analytical.

Mr. Reagan: They're both analytical, there's no question about it. I think Cooper and Barnes are a lot more alike than Cooper and White, other than personality-wise, other than their analytical effort. I think that White is probably much more analytical than Cooper, really. I used to get a little bit impatient with White, because he would analyze a thing, but I grew to understand him a lot more as I've been around him. You have to listen and hear him, because he goes pretty deep in his thoughts.

J. W. Reagan #1 - 58

Q: What do you remember of that great moment when you found out that you were one of the group to be commissioned and went to get a uniform?

Mr. Reagan: How could I say it? It was possibly the outstanding event in my life. It was sort of like a great dream coming true, a minor miracle or something, because I had always hoped to be a chief petty officer, a chief electrician's mate, if I stayed in the Navy long enough. I never even thought of becoming an officer.

Q: It wasn't in the realm of possibility.

Mr. Reagan: No. I knew I couldn't go to the Naval Academy. I knew all this, and I knew that if I stayed there long enough, I would hope to make chief. I thought about the Navy as a career, but when it came time, I thought of going to school and being a civilian.

Q: What was your first set of orders after you got commissioned?

Mr. Reagan: To Hampton Institute. They made me officer in charge of the electrical school. Sublett and I both were sent down to Hampton.

J. W. Reagan #1 - 59

Q: How challenging a duty was that?

Mr. Reagan: Not very. They had an instructor. I don't know what we did, really--just go around and look at the class. Maybe it was sort of a morale thing.

Q: Were you in any sense disappointed that it wasn't more of a challenge?

Mr. Reagan: Well, I didn't know. I felt that was kind of a temporary thing. My impression was that I didn't feel at first that the Navy really knew quite what to do with us, and while they were searching around, they said, "Well, Reagan and Sublett graduated from Hampton. We'll send them back." Something like that. You know, it was a little fun, but I don't recall anything terrifically challenging about it.

Q: Norfolk was still a heavily segregated area at that time.

Mr. Reagan: That's true.

Q: How did you live? Were you on base?

Mr. Reagan: We had quarters on the base, yes. I think we

J. W. Reagan #1 - 60

were only at Hampton three months, and Sublett got transferred out to San Francisco, and I got transferred to the Third Naval District. We both had gotten married.

Q: Where had you met your wife?

Mr. Reagan: I met my wife when I was at Hampton the first time. After I came out to California, she came out, and we got married. She didn't come back until I was in New York. She did come to Hampton just before, then went to New York with me. She became ill. She had tuberculosis. She had been a nurse. So we were in New York, and I had duty. I think my first duty was officer in charge under instruction of a PC.* Then later I was on the YTB with Jim Hair.**

Q: He was the skipper, I think.

Mr. Reagan: Yes.

Q: Why was he the skipper and not you?

Mr. Reagan: He was more experienced. But we used to take turns on and off.

Q: What sort of duties did the boat have?

---
*PC--patrol craft.
**YTB--a large harbor tugboat.

J. W. Reagan #1 - 61

Mr. Reagan: Well, we used to help with docking and undocking, break up ice floes up the Hudson River in wintertime, put water on fires on ammunition piers in New Jersey, and just generally be on call.

Q: Pretty versatile, it sounds like.

Mr. Reagan: Yes.

Q: Did you pick up the seamanship aspects of it pretty readily?

Mr. Reagan: I would say so. I don't think I was the greatest sailor in the world, but I think we did pretty well with the small craft.

Q: How large a crew did you have?

Mr. Reagan: We had about eight or ten people. I guess we had one of the greatest cooks in the Navy. I'm sure Jim told you about that. He was always way under budget, so we always had the best food.

Q: Many men who served in and around New York in the war

talked about how friendly and hospitable the civilians were, because they were grateful for what the Navy was doing. Did you encounter that sort of reception?

Mr. Reagan: Oh, we just were treated like kings. We met a lot of the top celebrities there, particularly the black celebrities. We hung around the Theresa Hotel, which was a big center of things at that time. Generally, we'd stay over there when we were in town. You'd meet people like Sugar Ray Robinson, Joe Louis, and others that were a lot of the top people.*

Everybody treated us just great, couldn't do enough for us. We met a lot of the top musicians. So that was really great in those terms. In fact, I think--I guess I spent of most my time in New York both times in the service: the first four years, and then after, I went back for that year. I was supposed to be back for a year in recruiting, and the Korean War came up. Each time, when I was shipped overseas, the war either just ended or was about to end while we were on our way there.

Q: What sorts of things did you and your bride do for entertainment during off-duty time?

Mr. Reagan: My wife, during the first tour, became ill
___
*Robinson and Louis were well-known professional boxers of the era.

almost immediately after we came to New York. She worked at Montefiore Hospital for maybe a month, and then she became ill, and she was ill all the time I was there. I was able to take her out once in a while on a weekend or something like that. In fact, our son was conceived just before I left. We went to Oxnard, California, first, just before we went overseas. So by the time I left the States, she was pregnant, and her problem had pretty well gotten taken care of.

Q: So you didn't have a concern about leaving her to go overseas, then.

Mr. Reagan: Of course, I hated to leave her, but she had improved so much that I knew it was just a matter of time that she would be well. By the time I got back, they had transferred her out of the care for her tuberculosis and had transferred her into another hospital, to watch and observe her during her pregnancy, just before delivery, for three or four weeks or so. I was back for the birth.

Q: Before we get to that, maybe we could talk about your time overseas at the end of the war.

Mr. Reagan: I was made an operations officer with a

J. W. Reagan #1 - 64

logistics support company. I guess a lot of fellows had that similar experience. I think our pattern of assignments was sort of similar, except for Hair and Baugh. I went to Guam first and then Okinawa with this logistics support company. The war ended when we were on our way over there. In fact, the people on Okinawa had just gotten over a big typhoon when we hit there. There was not a lot to do. We went to Okinawa. I don't remember whether we went to Guam first or Okinawa first, but I wound up being on the base. I was working with the construction battalion. I'm not quite sure what they had me doing there, but I know that morale was quite a problem at that time. The skipper called all the officers in together and wanted to know what he could do about morale. I think they were having adjutant general inspection, going around all the bases, finding out why morale was so bad and what could be done.

During the time I was on one of these islands--and I think it was Okinawa--all the camps were muddy. When it rained, just mud and water, so I recommended that they build a great big concrete slab, the size of a football field, and have a basketball court, badminton courts, shuffleboard, and things like that. I remember well the chaplain saying, "What we need is a chapel here, and that will take care of the morale." Somehow I won out. They built a slab.

J. W. Reagan #1 - 65

When the inspector came through, everybody was in their huts and everything, nothing going on except in our camp. It had stopped raining, but everything was muddy and flooding. All our guys are out there playing basketball and shuffleboard, just sitting around talking on a dry concrete slab. So the skipper got pretty high marks for that, and he was pretty happy he did.

I don't remember anything else that was too remarkable about that first tour over there.

Q: I think a big morale problem was the fact that the war was over, but the guys still weren't home.

Mr. Reagan: That was definitely a problem. The guys were shooting over our heads when the officers would be down in front looking at the movies. We'd have these raids at night going through all the huts and everything, trying to find weapons and all that sort of stuff.

Q: How long did you stay over there in that tour?

Mr. Reagan: That was the fall. I think I was on my way back for release in January '46. That's when I got out. Then, of course, I told you about the hospital and about my wife.

J. W. Reagan #1 - 66

Q: At what point did you return to Montana State to play football?

Mr. Reagan: I'd been working for sort of a boys' club agency there up in Harlem. About April or May of '46, Coach Doug Fessenden called and asked me to come up for the summer. He wanted to get together with me on being the T-formation quarterback.

Then the baby was born, and we decided that Lillian would go to Kentucky with her parents and then join me out in Montana that fall.*

Q: Were you covered by the GI Bill at that point?**

Mr. Reagan: Yes. In my last year, I didn't have to work so much.

Q: Was there any problem fitting back in, after the layoff from studies?

Mr. Reagan: No. In fact, I did better than ever. I think a lot of the veterans did.

---

*The child was John Walter Reagan, Jr., born 25 March 1946.
**The GI Bill, or Servicemen's Readjustment Act of 1944, provided educational assistance and other benefits to all veterans honorably discharged with six or more months of active service after 16 September 1940.

J. W. Reagan #1 - 67

Q: More mature.

Mr. Reagan: Yes. I went ahead and continued with economics and sociology, and I liked Mike Mansfield, so I took his class in political science.* I took a law course. In a year and a half I graduated. Then I had an offer to play with the Chicago Rockets, a new professional football team.** Then I had an offer to play up in Canada, which looked pretty good, so I decided to go up there. I didn't like the contract from the Chicago team. The one up in Canada was okay, so I went up there.

Q: Did you suffer any in the football skills from having this five-year layoff?

Mr. Reagan: I was always in great shape. I did well. I don't think I was any superstar or anything my last year, but I did well. I had my moments, at least good enough to get offers from the Canadian League and new teams that were starting up. I don't recall having any physical problems. At the end of the first year up in Canada, I got hurt. The blocking wasn't so good, two or three yards on each side of the line of scrimmage. I was trying to gain a few extra

---
*Michael J. Mansfield taught history and political science at Montana State University, 1933-42. Later he served in Congress, first as a representative and later as a senator, 1952-76. In 1977 he became U.S. ambassador to Japan.
**This team was in the All-America Football Conference, which merged with the National Football League in 1950.

yards and got hit by a ton of beef while my knee was extended. So that laid me up for three or four games, but I finished the year. Then I decided that probably I'd had enough.

Q: Which team did you play for?

Mr. Reagan: Winnipeg. We played for the Grey Cup and lost by a rugby, by one point. I threw the touchdown pass to win the game, and the officials said I was over the line of scrimmage, that I'd crossed it. They had some film after the game that didn't show that.

Q: They didn't have instant replay then.

Mr. Reagan: No. But that was controversial. I had fun up in Canada, and I think I might have stayed up there longer, but I had my wife up there by this time. She had had a taste of California, and it was just too cold for her in Canada.

Q: I think your size would have been a real asset in the backfield.

Mr. Reagan: I was a pretty good size back for that time.

I'd probably be an ordinary size back right now.

Q: How tall are you?

Mr. Reagan: Six-one and a half. I was always about 195 when I was playing. Taking my playing career as a whole, I had a few great moments.

Q: Are there any that you especially remember?

Mr. Reagan: This was a funny deal. This was a game against Texas Tech. This was the last time we played. They came to Montana. As I mentioned earlier, we weren't going to return because I wouldn't have been allowed to stay with the rest of my team.

During the game, the center was centering the ball to me direct, and the ball was off, and it went ten or 20 yards up the field. I ran, got the ball, I scrambled, and I kept running around. I remember running for it, jumping straight up in the air, and rifling a pass about 40 yards or so, and a receiver caught it. For some reason, that thing sticks in my mind. I just thought sure as hell that I was going to get caught back there. That's just an outstanding play that I remember.

Other than that, I remember our moral victories out here in California. I remember playing more for the people

I played against. I played against Waterfield.* I don't know if you remember him. He was a quarterback at UCLA, and they beat us 7-6, which was a moral victory for Montana.

Q: Waterfield was with the Rams for quite a number of years.

Mr. Reagan: Yes, and I also played against Albert of Stanford.** We always did pretty well, except when we'd get worn down, because we didn't have any depth. We played against a guy from Gonzaga that was with the Packers for quite a while, and that was the game Paul Robeson was at. I think we were both from Chicago, Tony Canadeo. I don't know if you know who he was.

Q: I've heard the name.

Mr. Reagan: Yes. We both were from Chicago, I think, and there was a big, big hullabaloo about Reagan and Canadeo, and we beat them. So I had some nice memories.

I remember my first year of eligibility, we played the Marines here in San Diego, and they had all these pros and

---
*Bob Waterfield was a noted quarterback in college and later played for the Cleveland Rams and Los Angeles Rams in the National Football League.
**Following his time at Stanford, the left-handed Frank Albert was a quarterback for the San Francisco 49ers of the National Football League.

J. W. Reagan #1 - 71

everybody. I just had one hell of a great day running off tackle, so I kept hearing, "Stop that nigger! Stop that nigger! What's the matter, buddy?" That was a great day for me. I had a lot of great moments in athletics.

When I was wrestling, I won city and state heavyweight championships in high school and the state university championship in Montana. There was only Montana and Montana State, so that wasn't a big deal. I had some pretty good times.

Q: Did you ever have any regrets that you hadn't picked one of the Big Ten schools?

Mr. Reagan: I have thought about it at times. Our whole backfield was recruited to go to Michigan.* I remember Rudy Smeja was an end, Ceithaml was the quarterback, Wally West, and myself. I think the three of them went up there, and two, Smeja and Ceithaml, were starters at Michigan. I kind of gave a lot of thought to that, but I don't regret it. Now I don't.

Q: What happened after your wife decided that Winnipeg was too cold?

Mr. Reagan: We came back to California. Then I faced the
_____
*University of Michigan, Ann Arbor, Michigan.

real world. I worked in a liquor store for a while, then I worked in the insurance business. At some point we bought a home.

Q: What was your degree in that you got from the University of Montana?

Mr. Reagan: Economics and sociology. The Korean War came in June of '50, didn't it?

Q: Yes.

Mr. Reagan: October of '49 is when I heard from the Navy Department, asking me to come back. Dennis Nelson told me that he was working on a recruiting program for blacks, so I said, "Okay." I actually got orders to report to the recruiting district in New York. Of course, war came up that following June, and that's why I stayed on active duty another four years, most of that in recruiting.

At the end of the war, this time I was in amphibious group, a boat unit that was headquartered here in Coronado and also at Camp McGill down below Yokosuka in Japan.

Q: How long were you in New York on the recruiting duty?

J. W. Reagan #1 - 73

Mr. Reagan: Almost three years.

Q: That was a specific effort to recruit blacks, wasn't it?

Mr. Reagan: That's right, yes. However, when the war came up, my main duty became signing shipping orders and swearing in people, because they were recalling everybody.

Q: Were you at the Third District headquarters?

Mr. Reagan: Yes, first down on Church Street and then we moved over to Broadway.

Q: Were you a lieutenant by then?

Mr. Reagan: Yes, I made full lieutenant then.

Q: Had you drilled any at all in between the periods?

Mr. Reagan: It wasn't until after that tour that I got involved in the drilling unit in Compton. But I think there was kind of a significant thing during the Korean situation. The boat unit was one of the commands in what was known as a beach group. The boat unit had about 12 officers, including myself, another full lieutenant, and the skipper, who was a lieutenant commander or commander. The exec left, and the skipper had to select between the two senior-grade lieutenants there. I was the only black guy in the unit. In the various companies, groups had betting pools about who he was going to select. He called me in, and he said, "You're my man." So that was interesting, because I'm not quite sure that a few years prior to that, that that would have happened, but it might have.

Q: The Navy was still not doing a great job for blacks even then.

Mr. Reagan: I know. It was still quite a bit second-rate. But we had a good time. I guess I was a good preparer for inspections, because we had an admin and engineering inspection there, and we got top marks. That was my job, of course, as exec, to prepare the unit for that. Other than that, we'd go out looking for pilots who had gone down in the Sea of Japan. We did a lot of joint exercises, landing exercises, in taking people off the boats and off the transports, with the Army and Marines and Air Force.

Q: Was it a training type of mission?

Mr. Reagan: I suppose you would call it training, yes.

J. W. Reagan #1 - 75

The exercises were very serious, though. I mean, they went through the whole thing just as though it was war--with the waves and all that--to establish and secure the beachhead.

Q: Did you get to the Korean area itself?

Mr. Reagan: I did not. We had a unit up in Korea, but the headquarters people never went over there.

Q: Did you have a greater sense of fulfillment in that duty than in recruiting because it was more related to the war?

Mr. Reagan: No question about it. See, back in 1944, I thought that we would finish this officer candidate school, and I was going to get on a big ship as a division junior officer and go that whole route. So I had a little disappointment about that. I was always asking to be transferred to an active theater, and that never came about. Again, even the Korean situation was almost over by the time I even got a chance to go. I should be thankful, I guess now, that I never got hurt. But at the time, when people started telling me war stories, I didn't have a war story.

Q: Part of that is strictly a matter of luck. For

example, Sam Gravely did get assigned to the Iowa that went to that area.*

Mr. Reagan: Yes, he did.

Q: Was there any sort of informal network or organization among the few black officers that were in the Navy then?

Mr. Reagan: I don't recall any. If I ran into somebody, it was totally incidental. I think we were in such diverse places and everything.

Q: When Nelson got you back on active duty, did you keep in touch with him after that?

Mr. Reagan: Oh, frequently. I'd stay at his home in Washington when I had to go down there for something. He would stay at my mine when he came to New York, and we went out together, and things like that. We'd talk about different things. I was interested in his experiences as a career officer.

Q: He was the defender of the faith there for a while.

---

*Samuel L. Gravely, Jr., was a lieutenant at the time of his service in the Korean War. His recollections of service in the battleship Iowa (BB-61) are in his own oral history.

Mr. Reagan: Yes, he was. Then he retired and went to work for the Urban League. After I lost my son, I got out of business for a while, because I was trying to build it for him.*

So I got out of business, and then I began, through Nelson--Nelson's kind of woven through my life--I got into the Urban League business and stayed for four or five years.

Q: What did you do after the Korean War ended?

Mr. Reagan: After the Korean War ended, I came back to Los Angeles. We had a home here then. I worked for the State of California Department of Employment and was advancing rather rapidly in that--everybody was saying more rapidly than a lot of people had seen. I was security officer 1, and in a year, as soon as I could take the test or do whatever you needed to do, I was security officer 2.

At the same time, I was working part-time in real estate. I got ahold of a great big deal that was complicated, and I quit working for the state. In real estate, except for the time after I lost Skip and went to work for the Urban League, that's what I've been doing and still do.** I've tapered off. I'm not doing commission

---
*Reagan's son was killed in the Vietnam War.
**Skip was the nickname of John Walter Reagan, Jr.

J. W. Reagan #1 - 78

sales so much. We've got some investments with a partner in several income units, and most of my time is in managing that. Until the new tax law of 1986 passed, we were pretty aggressive in acquisitions. We want to kind of see how things go.

Q: What was your work with the Urban League? What did you do there?

Mr. Reagan: When I went over there, I was the deputy director and director of employment for the Los Angeles area. I had about three or four jobs. Then the executive director left, and we had a new fellow come in, and he wanted his own deputy. There had been an effort to establish a league in Pasadena, and so, because there wouldn't be any big problem with them doing that, I asked for that job. So I established the Urban League in Pasadena. I stayed with that for about four years.

Q: What sorts of projects were you involved with on behalf of the League?

Mr. Reagan: We set up job fairs. We related to all types of industry and business people, in developing jobs for people, and we started apprenticeship programs. I think we were at the forefront of the nontraditional jobs for women,

J. W. Reagan #1 - 79

to get them in "apprentice-able" trades. We did an educational project there in Pasadena that resulted in substantially fewer dropouts in the school system.

We ran a street academy school which actually recruited dropouts and gave them remedial education in a storefront setting. We did a brochure for the school district so that the general public could understand the policies and rules and regulations and that type of thing, because they didn't have any.

We put out a lot of fires at schools; we were able to negotiate things. For instance, one school just had to break up a riot because they didn't have any black girls on the cheering squad. We were able to get in there and talk to the principal and negotiate a situation where they would go ahead. They had some sort of a competition or something like that, you know, where a black girl was just out of it. We just simply got them to increase the squad and include her, but it took a long time. But it was a very serious situation. We were able to stop a lot of that kind of thing, street gangs, street groups.

That was the time, right after the Watts riots, when things were still a little hot and heavy.* We got the Urban League relating to the black militant groups and to working out things more programmatically rather than just

---

*In mid-August of 1965, blacks in the Watts section of Los Angeles rioted, resulting in 35 deaths and an estimated $200 million in property damage.

marching and picketing and things like that.

Q: Constructive outlets.

Mr. Reagan: Yes. We showed them that if that was not the whole ball game--developing and submitting proposals for positive action in social programs, that is, fostering employment, education, and so forth--that such things should be a significant part of it. I had a great personal part in this particular thing, which helped to attract funding and people, not only to the Urban league but also to other community organizations.

Q: It sounds as if you have gravitated through a series of leadership positions.

Mr. Reagan: Yes, I guess so. I guess I was probably on every board of directors, social agency and nonprofit group in the L.A. area for a while, president of many of them. We started a community housing development group. I had a variety of experiences along those lines.

Q: Did you have any involvement with Governor Reagan when he was here?*

---
*Ronald W. Reagan was governor of California from 1967 to 1975.

J. W. Reagan #1 - 81

Mr. Reagan: He had a black guy that worked for Lockheed on his labor relations board, and I never met Ronald Reagan while he was in office there, but I recruited this guy for our board of directors in Pasadena. I knew a lot of people in the administration. I just got teased a lot about it.

Q: I'm sure you did.

Mr. Reagan: In fact, we had a guy--it seems like after Wes Brazier got me on that staff in L.A., he fired everybody else, except one guy by the name of Brown.* So that's why I was doing so many jobs, or trying to. So they teased Brown and me.

Q: Brown was another governor.

Mr. Reagan: He was the governor that Reagan replaced, Pat Brown.

Q: You probably still get some kidding now that he's President.

Mr. Reagan: Oh, no question about it.

---

*Wesley R. Brazier, long-time executive director of the Los Angeles Urban League until his retirement in 1969.

Q: Was there ever any time during your service as a naval officer that you were not treated with the respect that an officer should be?

Mr. Reagan: I really don't think so. There was occasional avoidance, like the guy who crossed the street maybe to keep from saluting. I think the guy probably did it to keep from saluting a white officer too. As an officer, no. A couple of instances with enlisted guys, but it was like the bus deal--either time, I think, the resolution of the situation was something that I didn't feel that I had to lose any dignity or anything about.

Q: It sounds in general as if you had it easier than some of the other men in the Golden Thirteen.

Mr. Reagan: I hate to say that when we're in a group, but I think, "Geez, I ought to be able to feel like something like this happened." But I can't honestly say that it had. I don't know why, it just didn't.

Q: It's a matter of circumstance, in many cases.

Mr. Reagan: I think so. I was not at those places at those times.

J. W. Reagan #1 - 83

Q: This has been a very happy time for you, these last ten years, getting together with them. What are some of the highlights you remember?

Mr. Reagan: Oh, God. I'll tell you, the thing that sticks out in my mind is after all these years, even in the intervening years, I've seen maybe one or two black officers at a time. When we walked into this auditorium up in Monterey, and there was this big auditorium, big room, wall to wall black officers, I think at the time, captain on down.

Q: When was that?

Mr. Reagan: This was in '77.

Q: That was the first reunion.

Mr. Reagan: That was the first. It was the most amazing thing for me to see so many of these bright, young, beautiful, clean people, young people, at all ranks, all types of assignments. I think that's the thing that I'll remember longest. Because, you know, you're used to counting them on your hands and fingers and toes at most. Of course, you knew about Wesley Brown and knew about Gravely, and there were a few more people, but even though

J. W. Reagan #1 - 84

the percentage is still pretty low, in absolute numbers, I didn't realize that we really had that many people in the Navy.

Q: Were you treated as a celebrity by this group in Monterey?

Mr. Reagan: Ah, this group just made us feel like we were high up on a pedestal. It was just amazing to me. I guess I don't take myself that seriously, and I'm not sure any of the guys do. I know it was kind of a remarkable event that we were involved in in becoming the first group and all of that, but these guys were astounding, these young captains coming up and telling us, "We owe it all to you."

Q: I've seen that movie A Soldier's Story, and the ending, where all that the men there wanted was the opportunity to participate in the war, and that made such a world of difference.

Mr. Reagan: Yes, that's right. That's very true. I've just been so delighted to have this young flier, Buddy Penn, who was out here as the skipper of the North Island Naval Air Station over there.* Of course, Gravely, I just had to fly over to Hawaii to see him, when he had his

───────────
*Captain William Penn, USN.

change of command to take over the Third Fleet. I just am tremendously proud of what people are doing.

Q: I'm sure you have some memories of that 1982 reunion in the Kidd.*

Mr. Reagan: Oh, yes. Monterey was outstanding, but I think that was our most outstanding because we found Hair, of course.** The experience on the ship--it was a great little ship, too, you know. That was a remarkable, outstanding thing. That will be up there in memory for a long time.

Q: You told me, before the tape started, about the captain's reaction when Hair came on board.

Mr. Reagan: Yes. Hair is kind of bald. He resembles the Shah, he actually does, from a distance. The captain was kidding, of course, because he knew the helicopter was coming and bringing Hair. I think it just got to be a joke that the skipper got upset because he felt the Shah was

---
*From 13 to 15 April 1982, the nine surviving members of the Golden Thirteen held a reunion on board the guided missile destroyer Kidd (DDG-993) at sea in the Atlantic. See PH2 Drake White, "Golden 13 Together Again," All Hands, August 1982, pages 8-11.
**James Hair was lost to the rest of the group until 1982. He had spelled his name "Hare" in 1944 and thus was not able to be traced after he resumed spelling it correctly. He learned about the reunion on board the Kidd through a newspaper article and got back with the group.

J. W. Reagan #1 - 86

coming to take the ship back.*

Q: What was the reaction in the rest of the group when you saw him again after all those years?

Mr. Reagan: Oh, God! That's when we were competing to get to him fast enough to give him a hug, you know, and shake his hand and welcome him. I think it was just the most exciting thing, because we really didn't know what had happened to him.

Q: There were a good many photographs published from that reunion. The expressions on your faces of good fellowship and happiness are so striking.

Mr. Reagan: I know from some of the TV shows they showed later, it was kind of obvious. It was an amazing event. We were out to sea, and it was a great thing that the Navy did to get him there and get him on the helicopter, get him out to the ship, and give him back to us. You had to have a real great feeling about the Navy.

Q: How much do you continue to be involved in the Navy today?

---

*The Kidd was originally intended for the Iranian Navy. After the Shah's government fell in 1979, the ship was completed for the U.S. Navy.

Mr. Reagan: I think it's mostly emotional involvement. I sometimes get a chance to talk to individual kids about joining the Navy. I had a heart problem in '84, and then I had an accident. It was kind of uncomfortable for me to be driving down to Mission Valley, so I moved my office here. I thought I would slack off, and it's something that I'm still going to do. I firmly intend to get involved with the recruiting district advisory group here and to become more active. Some of the guys in the Golden Thirteen are really active in recruiting.

I just moved down here and got started in this market. I've really been working full-time. So now that I've gotten my work life stabilized, I want to really get involved at least with the recruiting service here. When I was in Los Angeles, I was involved with Wally Logan, commanding officer of the L.A. recruiting area, and his ARDAC--Area Recruiting District Advisory Committee. I also plan to renew my membership in the Navy League in the not too distant future.

Q: What other plans do you have for the years ahead?

Mr. Reagan: Well, I'm enjoying work, and I'm just going to keep on doing what I'm doing. My wife is a few years younger, and she's interested in her career with the telephone company. She gets up at 4:00 o'clock every morning and goes 75 miles up to Tustin to do that. I feel great, and I just feel like I'll keep on doing what I'm doing and enjoy it, wrestle and tussle with this old property.

Q: What reflections do you have, looking back 40 or 50 years, on the progress that the Navy and the nation have made in that time?

Mr. Reagan: Absolutely great progress. It's just like kids coming up in the last four or five years can't imagine a time without TV. You would have to have seen how it's been all along to recognize the difference. There's a lot to be done, but the progress, I think, has been just tremendous.

In meeting with the NNOA, I've found that the problem with the young officers now is that they don't know how to work within the system to compete for the spots that are out there.* They are spread out a little thin, and some of them are, some of them do, and some of them, I think, feel a little frustrated because they feel that their career ladder is not aligned and things like that. I think that's a job that NNOA can do, especially with older

---

*NNOA--National Naval Officers Association, a professional organization of black U.S. naval officers.

that's a job that NNOA can do, especially with older officers and officers who have been through the system. In almost every walk of our American life, there's a system that you have to work with. That's a part of the game.

Q: That TV analogy is interesting. I see that in my own young children. They never knew a time when there wasn't TV. The current generation of young black naval officers may not have an appreciation of what men like you went through.

Mr. Reagan: Yes, that's funny. The older guys say, "Tell these guys what it was like. They don't know." So we get up when they ask us to speak at conventions or something like that, and we go over the thing. They seem to appreciate it. They're always anxious to come up and talk to us about how it was and things like that. But that's true; they don't know anything about the degree of things that might be considered negative as it was in the past.

Q: It's amazing what you've spanned in the course of one lifetime.

Mr. Reagan: I just couldn't be more grateful for my life--all of it. I just marvel and sometimes wonder why I'm here and whether I deserve it. There are so many times when I couldn't have been, and I am. So I guess there must be a reason for it.

Q: You and your service have been a great legacy to today's generation, and this oral history is a marvelous legacy also to document what you've done. So I thank you very much for that.

Mr. Reagan: I thank you for taking the time and trouble to talk to all of us.

Q: It's not a trouble. It's been a great pleasure. I thank you, Mr. Reagan, for that opportunity.

Mr. Reagan: Good luck to you.

J. W. Reagan #2 - 91

Interview Number 2 with Mr. John Reagan
Place: Mr. Reagan's home in Encinitas, California
Date: Monday, 10 April 1989
Interviewer: Paul Stillwell

Q: I'm happy to see you again after an interval of a little over two years, Mr. Reagan, and I'd like at this point to go into some more detail. For example, we talked before just briefly about your mother and father, and I hope you could give me, perhaps, some more specific memories about your early life with them.

Mr. Reagan: Okay. Our family was an off-and-on family. My father was--I think I mentioned before--kind of a searcher. He was always searching for something better, so there were great periods when the family was not together as a family. I think it might have been a difference in personalities between my mother and dad. My dad was pretty much of a stickler on wanting my mother to be in the home. My mother wanted the family to always have something better, so she was always wanting to work. I think this was kind of a basic conflict between the two.

In my younger years, I'd say up until the time I went to college at Montana State University, there probably were about three to four separations in the family. The last period that we were together for a while--maybe two, three years--was in Chicago, and were fairly happy there. I think I mentioned the fact that we had a home. My dad made maybe $100.00 to $125.00 a month on a regular job and then through the part-time jobs.

About the time that I was to go to college, Montana State, on a scholarship, they were kind of on the verge of breaking up again. I said to them that I didn't feel that I should go away, that I wouldn't do very well thinking that my family's going to break up. You know how kids got to keep a family together sometimes. So they promised that they weren't going to break up, that they'd settle their differences and everything. But about midway through my freshman year there, I heard from my mother that she'd come out to California to live where her people were. It was kind of a trauma for me. That was the last time that they were together. Of course, we were practically grown then.

Q: Was that a problem for you and your brother and sister when you were growing up, this on-again, off-again relationship on the part of your parents?

Mr. Reagan: Yes, it was quite a problem.

After the war came up, the second year my dad was still in Chicago. I came back to work for a while before going in the Army Air Corps, I thought. But then, after I'd gotten to the Navy, he shortly thereafter left to go back to Texas. My sister went with him, and my brother stayed around Chicago with some relatives. I dearly loved both of my parents. I think my challenge in the situation was more that of trying to understand why they could not resolve their differences and not to blame either of them. It was just sad to me when they parted and a very happy time when they came back together.

Q: Well, a youngster growing up needs that influence of his dad.

Mr. Reagan: Yes. I am not sure of the effect these separations had on my sister, a year my junior, and my brother, who was nine years younger. In retrospect, I am certain that, in their own way, they experienced a great deal of unhappiness, as most kids do in divided families.

Q: How did you feel during those times when you didn't have your father's presence?

Mr. Reagan: Well, of course, we missed my father and I think what actually happened--I think my mother would try to do so much and make things so much better for us, and, except for not being around all the time, she would always be moving up a little bit, or trying to, and doing things for us. I don't know if that was her way of responding to the absence or not, but she never stopped going. So I guess the attention that she was able to give us somewhat made up for the absence of Dad. I know that it's possible, when the father's absent, for the kids to get pretty bitter or pretty depressed. But I don't remember having any really bad problems, emotional problems about it. It's just that I knew he wasn't there and not really quite why.

Q: Mostly disappointment.

Mr. Reagan: I guess disappointment, yes.

When I was away at college, I guess I was a little more mature at that time, but I was still hoping that they could stay together as a family. So I was being a little tricky by threatening not to go to college if they didn't stay together. I didn't know that that doesn't work, but it worked until they saw me off and got me started.

Q: But, also, when you get that old, you kind of realize that it's their problem and not yours.

Mr. Reagan: You certainly do. I had a job to do finishing school. As I said, my dad was still in Chicago, so when we went back on the first winter vacation, he was still there. I saw a bit of him, more so than my mother, although I think that second year I did get to see them, because we were--we played ball out here. I had a chance to visit with my mother and the folks out here.

It wasn't too big a deal. I had the newness of going to college and playing ball. And things like that, I guess, kind of made it less of a problem. I kind of resigned myself that this was probably a final break. Before that break, this was the longest time period that I remember my father being with us, that and in Flint, Michigan, several years prior to that.

Q: Did he support the family during these periods he was gone?

Mr. Reagan: I don't recall that there was a lot of support coming from him, although there might have been. I just don't recall that it was substantive.

Q: You may not have had any way of knowing.

Mr. Reagan: That's what I'm thinking, yes.

Q: But even so, it put a real burden on your mother.

Mr. Reagan: Oh, yes; oh, yes. She worked for some pretty famous people, and they were very helpful to her and to the family. We never really wanted for that much.

Q: Any famous ones that you remember?

Mr. Reagan: One was pretty notorious. She worked for Virginia Hill, who was Bugsy Siegel's girlfriend. They had a big home in Beverly Hills. In fact, I don't know if she was working for him when they got him through the living room window or not.* But around that time she had been working for him. I think maybe she had stopped working for Virginia and was working for somebody else out there. After they did Bugsy Siegel in, I think Virginia asked her to come back and be with her for a while.

Other than that, it was just very wealthy people, mostly out in the Beverly Hills area, that she worked for.

Q: That's the kind to work for.

Mr. Reagan: Oh, yes. Like I say, they were very good to her because she was pretty good in taking care of them.

Q: You mentioned that your dad was a stickler. What did you mean by that?

Mr. Reagan: Well, let's see now. For example, I used to

---

*Benjamin "Bugsy" Siegel was a thriving gangster until shot through a window and killed in June 1947. When he died, he was sitting on a sofa in Virginia Hill's opulent home.

sneak and smoke. I was pretty big, was a good athlete, but I smoked occasionally, especially off-season. It was all right with my mother. She caught me in the bathroom a couple of times blowing smoke out the window. She said, "You don't have to sneak and smoke. If you're going to smoke, smoke."

So I told my dad that, and my dad said, "Well, it's all right about what your mother said, but I prefer you didn't smoke around me. Just give me that respect." So, I mean, in things like that he was much more conservative than my mother.

Q: Any other examples that you remember?

Mr. Reagan: Oh, yes. I remember once that I played ball, as I may have mentioned, at Lindblom with a lot of Eastern European kids. One of the fellows had an uncle in Chicago that was an importer of, among other things, Czechoslovakian beer. This kid gave me a case of the beer at one time. I was a high school kid then--maybe a junior, something like that. So I brought it home and put a bunch of it in the refrigerator. Just before dinner this one day I took a bottle out, and I asked my dad if he would have a bottle with me. He said, "No, no thanks." I think it was not because he didn't drink beer, but the perception I have, the way I remember, is that he didn't want to drink the beer with me.

Q: He didn't want to condone your having any.

Mr. Reagan: That's right. And other things, I think, maybe like staying out late, like the kids do at that age. He'd say, "Well, you know, you ought to come in earlier. It's late to be out, 10:00, 11:00 o'clock, running around the streets." And he didn't want my sister to have company at the house, because he thought she was too young to be dating. Just by today's standards he was pretty tight, pretty conservative.

He didn't go to church much. My mother did.

Q: Was your mother much of a disciplinarian when you were younger than that?

Mr. Reagan: My mother did all the whipping. My father didn't do much whipping, but he was straight. My mother would give us little spankings about different things. Maybe my sister didn't clean up or do something that she was supposed to do.

Q: Well, that's very typical.

Mr. Reagan: Yes. I think once I took--I don't know what

cigarettes cost, probably a quarter--and bought some cigarettes once without asking her, and I think she tried to whip me then. But by this time she couldn't hurt me. So I just grabbed the strap, and I brought her to me and I said, "Mother, you know, this is time that you can talk to me about things." That was the last whipping I ever got from her.

She just wanted you to do well, and she was a very kind person, a very kind-hearted person. She wanted you to treat people right, to believe in yourself, and to believe that you could do anything you wanted to do. She had a very outgoing, wonderful personality.

Q: You suggested that before you got to Lindblom and Englewood, you fell in with the wrong crowd. I wonder if that was a reaction to your dad not being there.

Mr. Reagan: I think it was, quite a bit. This was in another section of town.

Q: Where was that?

Mr. Reagan: This was in Chicago's east-southeast side: in terms of streets, Prairie Avenue, Indiana Avenue, around in that area. I was quite young, although I was large for my age.

Q: How old? Ten, maybe?

Mr. Reagan: I think I was about 11 or getting to 12 about the time we moved out to Englewood. But I'd say the troubles were around the ages of 9, 10, 11.

Q: Would you call it a street gang?

Mr. Reagan: Not so much as there are now, although there were definitely gang-type people. This was like, maybe, four, five, or six guys that hung out together. It was not so much as a gang but just a group of friends. The others in the group were all 14, 15, 16, around that age, and just getting in a lot of devilment. See an ice cream truck parked somewhere, they'd go grab some ice cream and go out in the park and eat it. And even earlier than that, I know guys used to take sweet potatoes off the vegetable stand, and the old guy would be running after them. Take them out to the park and roast potatoes and things like that. It seems like I was always running behind these guys or running right on the tail end or something. They would say, "Well, kid, come on," or something like that. I was just following them around.

Q: Peer pressure can be quite an influence.

J. W. Reagan #2 - 101

Mr. Reagan: Yes. As I think I mentioned before, we got out to Englewood, and people were interested in athletics and that sort of thing, so I kind of grew out of the things I had been doing.

Q: Do you think that move prevented you from getting into scrapes with the law? Do you think it might have led to that, had you stayed?

Mr. Reagan: Oh, I'm certain it would, because many of those fellows got involved with the law and more adult-like crimes, and things of that type, and even dope and drugs at that time. I guess marijuana was the thing then--reefers they used to call them. So I heard about a lot of the kids getting in that kind of trouble. And now I just look back and consider myself very fortunate that I never got involved.

Q: Was it your mother's concern that led to the move, do you think?

Mr. Reagan: Oh, yes. There's no question about it, because she was always looking for a better place, better area, better neighborhood to go to. And most of the time she would. But Englewood was just great, and it did well by us up through finishing elementary school and getting started into high school and then, later on, going to college.

Q: You mentioned that you worked with your dad from time to time. Did you ever have any pleasurable outings, going to a ball game, or picnics, or that kind of thing?

Mr. Reagan: I believe that the most time I did have with dad alone was in working with him. He liked to fool around with cars, for example. He was always buying some old car. I remember once he bought a hearse. I think he wanted to be an undertaker at one time. He was going to fix this old hearse up and rent it out. And I used to go out and help him in the garage and things of that type. I don't know, maybe we couldn't afford it at that time, but we never went to any sporting events or anything like that. It was mostly work.

Q: Well, did he go out and throw a football around with you or a baseball or that sort of thing?

Mr. Reagan: Of course, in Englewood that was a part of life, and we were always doing it with the kids. But I don't remember my dad being that involved. As I would think about it now, his attitude was, "Well, I'm a father; I'm not a buddy."

Q: Well, that was probably his personality, from what I gather.

Mr. Reagan: I think so, yes. I think it really was. And just in a great sense Dad was self-made. His father was an educator, and his mother died when he was very young, and his step-mother was in education, too, so he got some vocational training. But he didn't stay home that much. As soon as he got out, he was away somewhere, even as a young person.

Q: Judge White told me that his parents put great stress on the importance of education. Did your parents?

Mr. Reagan: Oh, yes. Oh, yes. Both believed strongly in education. And, although they weren't able to say, "We're setting aside this much money for your education," because they never really had it, they were especially interested in my sister getting an education somehow.

One of the outstanding things that I remember about my dad is that we did have discussions about politics and philosophy quite a bit, and we were kind of on opposite sides there. My dad was a dyed-in-the-wool Republican and, of course, related well to the managers at the job. They were all Republican people too. And I had become sensitive to the Depression and things like that. And so we had some very deep discussions about the system. And, of course, I had a little book learning about the Socialist system, the democracies, and things like that. My leanings were toward the Democratic Party.

I also heard a lot of the propaganda, although I never got involved with the Socialists, as such, or the Communist Party, which was really going after people in the depressed areas a lot during the time I was growing up. But I remember recalling--and whether I got it from books or not--telling my dad that in our system we had quite a challenge, as opposed to the Socialist systems, where we were producing for profit. No matter how much need there was, when a thing became unprofitable, we would quit producing. Whereas, in those countries--the Communist and Socialist--their potential was unlimited in terms of production, because they, theoretically at least, could produce as long as their people had a need, without regard to profit. And I remember those kind of things, you know.

Neither one of us, I think, convinced the other too much about this subject. I wasn't saying what system was good or what system was better, but from someplace I got to thinking about this idea that there needs to be a floor but no ceiling. People should have the opportunity to go as high as they can in terms of wealth and achievement, but that there should be a floor below which no human being would fall in matters of food, health, shelter, and education. Those kinds of philosophical things we used to debate. That was a great part of my relationship with my dad, talking about politics and things like that.

Q: How well educated was he?

Mr. Reagan: My dad, as I recall, didn't have a great deal of formal education. He did go to embalming school. I don't know how far he got in his vocational studies. I think he may have had a year or two of college, or something of that type. My mother was not well educated either. I think she was only 14 or 15 when they got married. As I say, my dad read quite a bit, but they didn't have a lot of formal education.

Q: But did they talk to you about education as an avenue to success in life?

Mr. Reagan: Oh, there's no question about it.

My mother used to read to me a lot, I recall now, when I was very, very young. She used to read and show me pictures and things when we were down in Shreveport, Louisiana. She started me to school a little early. And I remember they used to take me to church, and they all thought I was going to be a preacher because I'd come back and almost repeat the sermon verbatim and tell them to say "Amen" and all that sort of thing.

There was a lot of motivation for my sister and me to go to school. I recall that my mother had my sister put in Catholic school because she thought she could get a better education there. So they were very much aware of the value of an education. Although I would say that I was not pushed into anything, when I myself got the feeling--particularly after getting out into Englewood--that I wanted to go ahead and go to school and perhaps win a scholarship of some type, then they were 100%--and especially my mother--behind me on that.

Q: Would they be inclined to harp at you to do homework, for example?

Mr. Reagan: I don't recall that they had to. I don't think I ever had any problem with homework. I did what I needed to do on my own, especially after starting high school. And I don't remember having any problems in grammar school either, except I used to play hooky once in a while.

Q: Did you enjoy reading for pleasure?

Mr. Reagan: Yes, I did; I used to love to go to a library.

I couldn't understand everything I read, but there were a lot of scientific subjects and things like that I just loved to look at, look at the pictures and learn as much as I could.

Q: The problem I have with my children is that they get hooked on the TV, and it's hard to get them interested in reading.

Mr. Reagan: Yes, that's a great loss too.

I guess I read selectively now. I just have to be interested in something. I can get interested in something about business. Once in a while, I'll pick up a book and not put it down. But my wife Dede's an avid reader, and I think most of our kids are.* But I tend to think and meditate and read things that are kind of current and of particular interest to me.

Q: Did you have an interest in business and financial things when you were growing up?

Mr. Reagan: I think I did, because my father had that bent; he always wanted to get a business of some kind started for the family. He never quite did.

I had a job with the state of California after I got

---
*Willita T. Reagan is John Reagan's wife.

out of the Navy, and I had a job with the Urban League for four, five, or six years. But most of it has been sort of independent contractor-type things, like real estate, which is strung throughout my life.

Q: What got you into that particular field?

Mr. Reagan: After that second tour in the Navy, I went back to school. I took some courses at Southern Cal, and I took a job with the state of California in the employment service. I got a real estate license because I had a friend that was in the business. I was progressing really well with the state of California, and I got ahold of a transaction in which an old man was losing some property. I started a relationship with him, seeing if I could help him save it in some way, if he wanted to try to sell it. It got to be a situation where every time I talked to him, he'd tell me about something else, some other piece of property. So there were a number of pieces of property. I got all involved in that deal, and so I resigned from the state, and I started just real estate full time. It's over 30 years ago.

We finally got most of his stuff sold, and I guess I've been kind of hooked with that side of the business for a long time, and I've had my own offices.

I had several interruptions in the career, but that's

basically how I got started in the real estate end of it. After I lost my son in Vietnam, I got a bit depressed. It was also right around the time that the riots and all this thing was starting in the 1960s, and the real estate in the area that I was working with was kind of dead.

Dennis Nelson was with the National Urban League at that time. And I was talking to Dennis about how I was feeling. So he said, "Why don't you take a job for a while? I think you'd do a good job for the Los Angeles Urban League because Brazier is letting some people go over there that he's unhappy with. I think you'd do a good job in his employment development department." So then I started to work for the Urban League and I had a few years with them.

And then I started the branch in Pasadena. And then Reverend Sullivan's program, OIC, they needed to get something started in the Los Angeles area.* So I accepted the job to establish one of their centers in the black community in south-central and in the east L.A. Mexican or "brown" community.

So we got that done and got everything finished ahead of schedule. We went for a nonprofit housing association, which we developed in Pasadena. After I helped get that established, I eventually got back into real estate, and

---

*Leon H. Sullivan originated the Sullivan Principle for business corporations in South Africa. OIC--Opportunities Industrialization Centers.

J. W. Reagan #2 - 110

I've basically been with that. I never quite got away from real estate, but I kind of changed directions in the way I was going with it.

Q: Was it rare for blacks to be involved in real estate 30 years ago?

Mr. Reagan: I know at the time there was an organization for blacks in the business, but we couldn't be licensed realtors at that time.

Just recently I've gone to work with a brokerage here, and a fellow that I like sold us two or three pieces of property. We decided to divest in the last year or so, so I put the properties over there with him. He said, "Well, why don't you bring your license?" He's been trying to get me to work for him for years.

I said, "Well, okay. We might as well, because it wouldn't be managing property and things like that." But since I've been with him--this has been since last September--I've joined the board of realtors here. I'm a realtor now, and I think back on those years when blacks couldn't be realtors, and, of course, it's been changed for several years now--since the Seventies, I believe. But that thought just comes to me that a lot of things happened back in those years that people don't even realize, that they just take for granted now. Anybody that's in the

J. W. Reagan #2 - 111

business now and wants to be a realtor, he goes and joins the realty board and meets their certain qualifications, and he's a realtor.

Q: Well, how did you operate in those years before you could be licensed?

Mr. Reagan: Well, I was licensed by the state as a salesman and later as a real estate broker. That could be done. But the board of realtors is a private professional organization. Like other private organizations, they practiced exclusion of minorities and females. I think these things all began to change with <u>Brown v. Board of Education</u>.*

Of course, there are a lot of people now that are not realtors. But why they wouldn't be, I don't know. But there are a lot of people that just have brokerages, but the realtor, the National Association of Real Estate Boards, is the top professional organization in the field. So there are both prestige and advantages from being in the organization, as well as being involved with the multiple listing service and the networking and all those sort of things.

I got my broker's license as soon as I had the two

---
*<u>Brown v. Board of Education</u> was a landmark case in U.S. judicial history. Decided by a 9-0 vote of the Supreme Court in 1954, it declared racially segregated schools to be unconstitutional.

J. W. Reagan #2 - 112

years as a salesman in the business, and had my own operation on and off for several years. But, basically, the real estate field has been my major interest.

Q: Something that you couldn't even have envisioned back there in Chicago.

Mr. Reagan: True. I really didn't know which way I was going to go. I think I mentioned when we were talking before, I thought I was going to be an entertainer.

Q: And then a doctor.

Mr. Reagan: Then a doctor, yes.

Q: Did your parents talk to you about the racial situation and ways to react to it?

Mr. Reagan: The way my mother related to that was not in a direct kind of a way. It was indirect, always saying to me, "You can be anything that you want to be." I don't think she even really concerned herself--as far as I can recall--with responding to whatever the racial situation was. Of course, we all know what it was, but she didn't describe it as something that would be a detriment or hold me back.

My dad, I don't recall him being that involved with it. It was just there, I guess.

Q: There were probably some things that you just experienced; they didn't have to be explained to you.

Mr. Reagan: That's true, you know, that's true. I can't say that I was not aware of it. Most of my schooling was on an integrated basis. There were differences between kids and things like that, but I don't remember it being a big issue in the home.

Q: How much awareness did you have of the situation elsewhere in the country, particularly in the South?

Mr. Reagan: Oh, great, great awareness there, because I lived through some of those periods when they had the lynchings, and even when I visited the South, I noticed a difference. Although the North was not totally unsegregated, we didn't have the signs "For Whites Only" and "For Colored Only."

When I was very young and riding the train, we had a certain car to go onto. So I was aware of the happenings in the South and how people were treated on such a blatant basis. Gradually, I became aware of the segregated

J. W. Reagan #2 - 114

patterns in the North, because there were areas that you just didn't live, and you just knew that. It wasn't something that was really a great outstanding issue at the time.

Q: You just adjusted as you had to, I guess.

Mr. Reagan: I think through the moderate amount of time that I've lived, I haven't come directly into a lot of confrontations. I've had some about eating some places, and I remember fighting that, and even in the South, where you were supposed to go in the back of the bus and things like that. I've had my little scraps about that, even in the service.

Q: How did you tend to react to those situations?

Mr. Reagan: I felt bad about it, and I'd get a little angry about it too. Fortunately, for the most part, in the instances that I had, there were other people around, whites that were supportive of my point of view on the thing. For example, just before leaving for Great Lakes in December of 1943, I was waiting to catch the ferry going from Hampton, Virginia, to Norfolk. It was very crowded on one side and not very crowded on the other, so the whites would fill up the black side, so both sides were equally crowded. And I would just get in line, and my line was going on the white side, and some guy wanted to get after me about that. I was saying, "The hell with it. You know, it's crowded over there and there are whites over there."

Then somebody else would say, "Leave the guy alone," or something like that.

I remember in Chicago I was walking to the beach one day in the summer of 1937 or '38 with my two best buddies. Some guy--he was nuts, I think--came up to us and said, "I see you guys looking at those white girls." He tried to start something because we were walking through a basically white neighborhood--that's all black now. And so we were waltzing around with the guy. He started to push my friend, and then I pushed him out of the way and pushed him up against a car. This guy was saying, "Look what he did to me," trying to get the white people incited. But nobody paid any attention to it, so we just walked on.

You feel a little anger and a little bad about those things. I know when I went down to the University of Illinois to participate in the wrestling championships, I went into a restaurant to have a bite to eat and they wanted me to sit in the back there. It's a university town.

But I'd say for the amount of time that I have lived, those incidents were relatively few. But they were enough

J. W. Reagan #2 - 116

to let me know that there was a lot of segregation and prejudice: more open in the South, more subtle in the North, but pervasive throughout.

Q: Do you think the prejudice you saw had any influence on your being interested in learning about Communism, because it supposedly was a more equal type system?

Mr. Reagan: I don't think there was ever any--I don't know whether you'd call it danger or not. I think what knowing about Communism, Socialism, Fascism, and other systems did was give me a feeling of wanting to make things better in America. I didn't have any feeling for the system particularly, as such, but for the feeling of having things more equal. The fortunate thing about it for me, I guess, was that blacks and other minority people were not the only ones that felt that things should be better as citizens of the country.

I think that I always had the feeling it was a great country. I'd just like to be more a part of it. It wasn't anything wrong with the country, but that part of it was not a good thing. I recognized that without the country making some changes that way, a lot of these principles of Communism and other systems would have a tendency, probably, to attract a lot of people. And I'm sure they did. Maybe there were a lot of people that felt the way I did about racial discrimination but went farther than I did toward the Socialist and the Communist systems. But I think for the most part, black Americans have basically just wanted to be Americans with equal opportunities to participate and contribute.

Q: Did the Communists ever try to recruit you?

Mr. Reagan: They did in my neighborhood. I remember they used to have guys and nice-looking young ladies come around and say, "We're having a picnic and music and dancing over here," at some park or something. A lot of the guys did go. That came to haunt a lot of guys, because somehow it was found out that they had fooled around with these groups. I'm just not quite sure why I never got involved. I just didn't. I don't remember saying, "Well, if I go get involved in this some day I might want to go in the Navy and be an officer and they'll come back." I didn't have an idea of anything like that. I guess the group of us that did not go or get involved in those things was the group that I happened to be with.

Another incident is when I left school that winter quarter because I thought the Air Force was going to call me. I went to work in a meat-packing plant. It was not a union shop, but there was a little old man there that was trying to get it organized. He recruited me. And I'd studied about the labor movement a little bit. So that sounded a little exciting to me. So I said, "Okay, I'll help you out," and we started to organize the plant. I remember the management or supervisor saying this guy was a Communist and all this sort of thing. I didn't see anything that I could detect as Communist. He was a hard-working little guy. We did our work, and we were getting the shop organized. I don't know how far that went, because I went down to join the Navy to avoid getting drafted.

I don't recall ever getting really close to being involved in the party. But I know there were a lot of efforts made in and around me and about me. I think there was a little cell out there on the Montana State campus somewhere, but, of course, I was really more involved in athletics and things like that. So I really never got involved in the party as such.

I told you before about the time I met Paul Robeson at a football game. I know he lived in Russia, but I don't remember seeing anything about him personally pushing Communism as such. But, of course, he got the label.

Q: That certainly haunted him.

Mr. Reagan: Yes, it really did. I think maybe in his last year or two, that sort of thing kind of subsided for him,

J. W. Reagan #2 - 119

and I think he was back in the United States.

No, there's nothing on my part that I can recall that got me involved with that sort of thing.

Q: How was President Roosevelt perceived in the black community in the Thirties?*

Mr. Reagan: Well, I know I was for him, and I think the black community was, too, in general, because there had been some pretty hard times, and he gave some promise of relief. I know there were a lot of young people who went to the CCC and felt a little dignity.** They had some kind of jobs or some sort of independence. He got some programs together, and, as far as I'm concerned, they pulled the country out of a pretty tough situation.

I think he was well liked in the black community and, I guess, a lot of the country as a whole.

I'm sure that there was still a conservative side of the issue. There were still a lot of "haves" in the country, but a lot of people had lost a lot, lost everything.

---
*Franklin D. Roosevelt was President of the United States from March 1933 until his death in April 1945. In the early years of his administration, he oversaw the creation of many organizations and agencies to deal with the problems resulting from the Great Depression.
**CCC--Civilian Conservation Corps was one of the Depression Relief agencies. Its purposes were twofold: to provide useful employment for young people and to aid the environment through such measures as planting trees.

Q: It would be interesting to know how your father, with his management viewpoint, reacted to Roosevelt and his reforms.

Mr. Reagan: Oh, well, as I recall, I know that we were having discussions about that time, 1932.

Q: That's when he was elected.

Mr. Reagan: That's right, get Hoover out of there.*

I'd say my dad was not a Roosevelt man, because a long time ago I guess blacks, because of Lincoln, were Republicans.**

Q: Right.

Mr. Reagan: And that was probably a tradition for him. But along about that time, I think that there was this conservative-liberal type thing beginning to emerge, and I think he was on the side of the conservative, possibly

---

*Herbert C. Hoover was President of the United States from March 1929 to March 1933. He is generally viewed as believing that private society, rather than the federal government, needed to provide the solution to the problems of the Depression.
**Abraham Lincoln was President of the United States from March 1861 until his death in April 1865. In 1862 he issued the Emancipation Proclamation, freeing slaves in the United States.

because a lot of the influence from his job. I know he was deathly against welfare, any kind of welfare, and just kind of a total conservative. A lot of our arguments were about that, that the Republicans seemed to be for the rich people, and the Democrats seemed to be wanting to help the poor. Of course, there were a lot of rich Democrats, but you find out a lot of the things that were done were political, of course, not so much from the goodness of heart.

I think he had feelings about giveaway, about charity; he thought everybody ought to just work and better themselves the best way they could. There's nothing wrong with that, but I don't think he ever gave much thought to structural problems within the system that tended to keep some people down. I used to argue with him, because I heard it somewhere that in the South--it was fine that even in the union movement there--the South was great if the whites could be paid a nickel more an hour than the blacks, you know, just so they got something more. We had all of those kinds of philosophical things going. Sometimes I would be the devil's advocate, whether I believed what he was saying or not, just to try to show that I was thinking about the thing too.

Q: One of the metaphors that was used at that time, not that it was a giveaway, but priming the pump. You put some money into the system so people can help themselves.

Mr. Reagan: Yes.

Q: Do you have any recollections--we touched this just very briefly the last time--about your time in Louisiana and in Michigan?

Mr. Reagan: I was only a year older than my sister. We must have been around three or four years old when we went to Shreveport. I guess my dad had gone somewhere, and my mother moved us to Louisiana, where her mother and her sisters were. The biggest thing I remember there, she worked for a lady named Styles, and the Styles family had cottages for their help. Their house was kind of up on the hill. You walked down a big set of stairs, and then there were these neat little cottages where we lived.

That's the time I remember when we would go to church. I was very interested in what the preacher was saying, and I could remember a lot about what he was saying.

I remember walking to school in the mornings with my little knickers. I was still quite young at that time. I remember relating to my grandmother, who was the matriarch in every sense. She was Mrs. Styles's seamstress; in fact, she sewed for most of the wealthy people. Even though my mother and her two sisters were young adults, my grandmother laid down the law about courting and other aspects of behavior.

My mother was the oldest child. After her came her two sisters and my uncle, who was the youngest. Uncle Hal was kind of a free spirit; he was a very nice-looking man. When I was just small, I remember that he used to tell me how to talk to girlfriends and things like that, because he got a big kick out of it. He would tell me to say, "Listen here, Mary. Come over here, Mary, and do this and do that." Uncle Hal left; he was the first to go to California.

The only other thing I remember is a time when I was playing with my sister, and I fell on a fish bone. I got a three-inch scar across my knee and had it a long time. It used to be such a wonder to me how a fish bone could do that to me.

Q: Did you like to be outdoors quite a bit?

Mr. Reagan: I just loved it. I know I visited my grandfather in Texas when I was maybe six and seven. We may have even left to come to Chicago then. My grandfather was there in the big house all by himself at this time. He used to get dressed and put on his straw hat and get in his little yellow convertible, A Model Ford, so he could go to make his rounds of vocational schools. When I was there, I just took off. I'd go out in the woods and climb trees and pick fruit and just play Robin Hood by myself. It was just kind of a wonder thing, and I just loved it.

Q: What was the motivation in going to Michigan?

Mr. Reagan: Well, okay, my dad brought us from Shreveport, Louisiana, to Chicago. He found a place and he was working for, let's see--he might have been working for Jelke Margarine then. He was working for somebody; I'm not sure who it was. But then he left to go to Michigan, and there he got a job with Buick and he called, and we left and we went to Michigan with him. We had a few years there in Michigan, where my brother was born, and Dad had a pretty good job working for the Buick Company in Flint. So that's why we were in Michigan.

Q: Do you have any recollections of the family life there?

Mr. Reagan: I remember we had a pretty good size house, and we used to rent rooms to two or three musicians. And I remember that they used to clean their reeds and try to teach me how to play notes on the saxophone or trumpet. And my mother even went out and bought me a trumpet. And I was taking lessons in school, as I recall. And then things got tough again. The family broke up again, and I guess my mother sold the horn or pawned it or something. I remember liking Flint, and I remember running around, and I remember my best friend and I were up in a cherry tree picking cherries and he fell out and broke his arm.

I remember once I had a very sad experience. There was a bird, a little sparrow, that was getting ready to take off. I was in the backyard, and I picked up a wrench or something and threw it ahead of him. He ran into it--at least I hit him. The poor thing fell down to the ground, and that was one of the saddest things in my young life. I guess that's why I remember that. It was such a sad experience. I guess I was trying to hit him, but the fact that he fell and that he died, you know, was kind of a trauma to me.

Q: Were you old enough at that point to appreciate a difference in racial treatment between Michigan and Louisiana?

Mr. Reagan: No. I really was not at that time. I don't recall running into it that much in Louisiana, if at all, and really not in Michigan. Everything was family in Louisiana, and family-oriented type things. I do remember that there were parties once in a while, and there was the home brew and things like that.

One of my aunts--the youngest daughter was married to a baseball player named Talmadge. When we were in Shreveport, I remember him coming in in his baseball togs and his cleats and things like that, and all sweaty. And that impressed me a bit.

Q: Was he in the old Negro league?

Mr. Reagan: Probably, because he had the uniform. He wasn't rag-tag, and I think probably I saw one or two games. But I was impressed with him.

I also remember about Flint that that was one of the periods where I used to love to go to the library, and I'd look at these technical books and all these pictures, astrology and so forth. I'd just sit in awe looking at these things, but even if I could read them, I couldn't understand what they were saying. But I could pronounce the words, or think I was pronouncing.

Q: What sort of work did your father do for Buick in Flint?

Mr. Reagan: To the best of my knowledge, he was in some part of the assembly work. But I'm not certain of that.

Q: What sorts of heroes did you have when you were a

youngster?

Mr. Reagan: Oh, God. Let me think about that. Well, I certainly liked the entertainers. Cab Calloway was a great, great man for me; Duke Ellington; the entertainers.* I think probably Franklin Roosevelt was, although I was a little older at this time. I can't think specifically who else was. But I know as a group, some of the entertainers and movie stars and those kind of people were people that I kind of looked up to.

Q: Were movies a popular form of entertainment for you?

Mr. Reagan: Yes, whenever I could go. This was not until we were back in Chicago again, I guess maybe when I was around eight or nine years old.

I don't know. I guess my heroes were people of the times at that stage of the game.

Q: Were there any people that you would describe as role models for you?

Mr. Reagan: Well, a fellow named Arnett Eskridge. George Edwards was a great athlete out in Englewood. Arnett was a

---

*Cab Calloway (1907-   ) has long been a popular black singer and dancer; Duke Ellington (1899-1974) was a noted black jazz composer, pianist, and band leader.

scoutmaster and just a good influence. A fellow named Joe Robeshau helped organize baseball teams and things like that in our neighborhood, and he was an employee of the Catholic Youth Organization. I think Joe had a great influence on my mother sending my sister to Catholic school. And I converted at one time. They were mostly the local people, as I recall, at that time.

Q: You mentioned an English teacher who was very helpful to you.

Mr. Reagan: Oh, yes, Mrs. Edwards. She probably made everyone feel like this, but I felt that she paid special attention to me, and she was encouraging me and trying to influence me that I should be a leader and set an example, and just always seemingly motivating me to do well. I remember I used to like to write essays and things like that. I don't know any particular reason why she would. Maybe she just wanted to make me feel good because when I went to Lindblom, there were not a lot of black students, Negro students. Maybe she was just trying to motivate me along those lines. This is in retrospect, but she was one of the people that I think about that tried to be a positive influence for you and tried to motivate you to do your best.

Q: How good a student were you?

Mr. Reagan: All the way through, I was an above-average student. We had a large class, of course, in Lindblom, but I guess I graduated in the upper quarter. I was categorized a student athlete in college. I don't know percentage-wise where I stood in the freshman or sophomore class. Like most people, after I got back from the service the first time, I went back to finish school. I was probably a lot more serious about it and did really well in the final year there.

Q: Were there people who encouraged you as you were coming along in your leadership qualities?

Mr. Reagan: I'm not sure, per se, that I could call anyone a guru or something like that, that sat down and said, you know, "Here's the way you need to go to become a leader." I think my leadership situations just evolved by accident or circumstance. I always seemed to somehow be involved in a kind of a leadership-type thing.

Q: What would be examples of those?

Mr. Reagan: In work situations, let's say, I wouldn't be designated the boss or the leader or anything like that always, but I always seemed to have an influence in going toward whatever goals or whatever our objectives were without, as I recall, trying to put myself in that position.

Q: Well, for example, how did you get into the leadership role in that union organizing effort at the meat plant?

Mr. Reagan: I think, number one, is that in college I had economics and sociology courses, and I read about the labor movement. The orientation was that in order to do away with the child labor laws and to have better working conditions and things of this type, labor had to organize its movement. So I had a part of that in my background.

I can't think of this fellow's name who was trying to recruit to help him, and I really don't remember anybody but he and I in there at first. I had the feeling that people are going to hold wages down so the profits would be better, so I was amenable to getting the better working conditions and people making decent wages and that sort of thing.

So that's how it was he and I got that started. I don't recall how many people we got to get into it, because I left fairly early, but I was involved in the organizing part of it and talking to people. Eventually, then, it was organized, but I don't know what part we had played in that

J. W. Reagan #2 - 131

plant overall.

Q: I talked to Mummy Williams in Chicago last year, and he said that he'd been told that his work on behalf of the railroad porters had an influence later on in him not getting commissioned*. But apparently that had no impact on your career.

Mr. Reagan: No, it did not. It did not. In fact, after I was commissioned I got to know Randolph pretty well, because his niece got to be a friend of mine, and we visited several times.**

Q: He was a very highly respected individual.

Mr. Reagan: Yes, he was. And, of course, he was instrumental in getting the sleeping car porters together as a union. I guess he had some background as a socialist in earlier years.

I'd say in any job that I've been on--I don't know whether you would call it a little center of influence or what--but I seemed to be selected a lot for different

---
*Lewis R. Williams was one of three black enlisted men who went through officer training with the Golden Thirteen at Great Lakes in early 1944 but did not become an officer.
**A. Philip Randolph (1889-1979) was probably the most noted black individual in the history of the American labor movement. He organized the Brotherhood of Sleeping Car Porters in 1925, organized marches on Washington in 1941 and 1963, and served as a vice president of the AFL-CIO.

J. W. Reagan #2 - 132

things. For example, when we decided to put a branch of the Urban League up in Pasadena, I was selected to do that job. And for some reason I was asked to get the OIC started there in the Los Angeles area. When we started the Non Housing Corporation in Pasadena, I was invited along with the group to be among the founding members. Somehow I was one of the first presidents of the organization after Sid Smith became the executive director; he really started it. I really was involved in so many organizations at one time, and at some, it seemed in a position of leadership. I was probably the president of three or four things like that. I don't have any particular explanation for it, really.

Q: Well, you obviously were perceived by others as being someone who could lead.

Mr. Reagan: I guess that was the perception, anyway.

Q: Well, I've heard something very similar from Graham Martin, for example. He said coming up in high school and college, he was president of this club and that club, and so forth.

Mr. Reagan: I guess some people go for those things, and for other people it just happens. I'm not saying that either one is good or bad. Maybe it'd be good if you did feel like, "Well, I guess I want to be the president of this," and go for that. I don't know.

I feel I've done most things that I wanted to do. If I really wanted to do something, I would go ahead and do it.

Q: Well, in that sense, you have fulfilled what your mother set out for you.

Mr. Reagan: That's true. About four or five years ago I decided, "Well, I'm going to get out of the commission business a while and acquire some property." Not that I had that much money, but I did, and in a year or year and a half my partner and I had gotten together 40, 50 units of property. Sometimes it may be that you just sort of set higher goals for yourself.

Then sometimes you wonder, "Well, maybe it was 30 years too soon," because the sort of things I used to dream about, guys are doing now. For example, I saw Central Avenue in Los Angeles going down, down, down. Then after the Watts riots in 1965, it was down about as far as it could go. I'd get together some guys, just kind of "BS-ing" a little bit, saying, "You know, I think we ought to buy up, we ought to try to get together and buy up Central

J. W. Reagan #2 - 134

Avenue and redevelop it." It wasn't too serious, but I'd been thinking about that. But then you see maybe eight, nine, ten years later starting at one end of Central Avenue, somebody buying it up and redeveloping it and improving it. So the things that you think about maybe seem like a little bit too much at the time, eventually somebody's doing them.

Q: We haven't talked much about you specifically as a wrestler. What memories do you have there?

Mr. Reagan: I don't know if it started on the playground out there in Englewood, but I started right as a freshman. I wrestled as a 175-pounder and a heavyweight. There were two of us, each 175 pounds, and we would switch off during my first year. Sometimes he'd wrestle heavyweight, and sometimes I'd wrestle heavyweight. We could both do either one. I think I won the city championship for two years, and then I was beat by a fellow named Lou Rymkus my senior year.*

I don't know if you ever heard of Lou Rymkus. Lou Rymkus went to Notre Dame and later played professional football. He was a professional coach. Lou was about 300

_____
*Louis Rymkus, a tackle, played his college football at Notre Dame University. Later he played professional football for the Washington Redskins in 1943 and the Cleveland Browns from 1946 to 1951. He was head coach of the Houston Oilers in 1960, the team's first season in the American Football League.

pounds and about six-six, or six-seven. The first year I wrestled him, he was a freshman, and I was at our school. I went to get a knee-dive on Lou, and he just fell on me. I thought he was going to pin me. Somehow I was able to bridge and get him standing straight up, just got him to go over and then he was too big to get up, so I pinned him.

I beat Lou for two years, and then the third year we were wrestling for the city heavyweight championship. And we wrestled at least four overtimes. And, finally, Lou won. So the coach at Tilden Tech at that time said, "I'm the coach for the city, and I'm taking you as my light heavyweight, and Lou's going to wrestle heavyweight." So that year I didn't win the city championship, but I went up and won the state 175-pound championship. That was the time, too, I had one of those experiences where I went out on my own one day while we were there and went in this restaurant. They wanted me to sit in the back.

Q: That was the one at the University of Illinois.

Mr. Reagan: Yes, University of Illinois, state wrestling finals. The guy that I wrestled was an Adonis, beautiful body and all the women and--oh, everybody was just hurrahing, and I understand his father was the mayor of the town. When I beat him, they said, "You're lucky to get out of town if you beat him."

J. W. Reagan #2 - 136

But wrestling was good to me, mainly for, I think, for keeping me in condition. I was in great, great condition. And so size of guys didn't mean too much to me at that time, although I was pretty big at that time, for a football back.

Q: You must have been very strong, also.

Mr. Reagan: Tremendously strong, yeah.

Q: Well, if you can handle a 300-pounder.

Mr. Reagan: Yes, it was no problem, and none of the heavyweights gave me too much of a problem either. None of the big linemen in football--of course, they're not all that big by today's standards. But I loved the contact.

Q: What other sports were you in?

Mr. Reagan: Wrestling, football, track, and, of course, boxing, but the boxing was just in Lindblom.

Q: What did you do in track?

J. W. Reagan #2 - 137

Mr. Reagan: I did enough to get a letter. I'd enter any event to get points. I'd maybe get a second because I really didn't train hard for track. I was in that mostly on a bet with a fellow that did only track. He was telling me how easy it was to play football, because everybody's part of a team. But he said you couldn't do it in track because that's individual. So I said, "Well, I bet you I can get a letter in track," so I just went out for track. And I'd get points, maybe, in the 440 relay or high jump. I think I even tried to pole vault, and other things like that. So I didn't specialize in anything in track.

Q: Yes, but it sounds like you're an extremely versatile athlete.

Mr. Reagan: I was versatile. I started late, because I didn't get into sports until we moved out in Englewood. All these other kids had been athletes on the playground, and all I was was a brash young kid from the east side of Chicago, saying I could do everything but actually couldn't do anything.

Q: Well, you must have been able to do something.

Mr. Reagan: Well, I started learning, and I probably had some natural ability that had an opportunity to come out.

Q: You mentioned that when you went up to Montana State, the rest of the backfield went to Michigan. But in a way you may have been better off, because Martin and Sublett, both of whom went to Big Ten schools, didn't get to play very much.

Mr. Reagan: That's true. It could have been. George Ceithaml was a quarterback for Lindblom, and he was a quarterback at Michigan. Rudy Smeja was really an end; little Wally West, hell of a nice high school running back, but I didn't hear much about anything he did at Michigan. I heard Smeja played and Ceithaml started, but I don't know much about West, really, so it might have been for the best. In fact, I think Smeja said something to me, "Why don't you go and be a big fish in a small pool instead of go and be a little fish in a big pool?" I guess that was a part of my going off to Montana. In addition, I always wanted to get far away from Chicago. That got me pretty far away, because I figured otherwise I'd be wanting to come home every time I got a chance.

Q: Well, Montana's pretty far from everywhere.

Mr. Reagan: It is. Believe me, it's even far from Montana.

Q: How was the racial climate there?

Mr. Reagan: My first run-in there, I think, was a Chinese restaurant. They didn't want to serve me. And, of course, I was going with the football players, and they weren't going to serve anybody if they didn't serve me. And downtown at the railroad station once, I think I took care of that on my own. They didn't want to serve coffee or breakfast or something. But I don't know, we just worked that out some kind of way. Other than that, everybody that I ran into or came into contact with was very good to me.

Q: How much did you play there?

Mr. Reagan: Oh, I was first string. I started most all the time. I didn't miss a game. I was hurt during one game, a charley horse or something. They just put me in the hospital to get me off my feet. Most of the time we were playing 60 minutes each game.

Q: What position did you play on defense?

Mr. Reagan: I was a cornerback, I guess.

Q: Defensive halfback they were called then.

J. W. Reagan #2 - 140

Mr. Reagan: Defensive halfback, right, and occasionally I played linebacker.

Q: Well, the fact that the coach knew your wrestling coach, I'm sure, gave you an advantage there.

Mr. Reagan: Yes, it did. There were other people from Chicago, including a senior center by the name of McDonald from Finger High School in Chicago. Joe Taylor, who was a freshman when I was, went with me on a basketball scholarship. Joe and I drove to Montana with Mac our first year. Coach Fessenden knew some of the Chicago coaches, and I guess he must have been in pretty good with them because there were about five or six of us there from Chicago. A couple of other Chicago guys had been there a little before us.

Q: What kind of scholarship arrangement did you have?

Mr. Reagan: We had everything paid, and we had some little part-time jobs that didn't amount to much time-wise. For instance, I worked in a finance office downtown. I'd go and sweep up and empty the trash every night. And then they had some kind of thing on the campus that we worked in. We made enough so that we'd have spending money, probably as much as the average guy on the street in those days.

Q: I've heard that one deterrent to athletes in that era taking scholarships was just the transportation cost to get to a faraway school. That must not have been a problem for you.

Mr. Reagan: No, it wasn't a problem. In fact, the first year we drove up with McDonald, and that first summer I bought an old Model A. I only paid 50 bucks for it, and although it broke down in Billings, we spent a few days with a friend up there who was also a freshman, Paul Billings. We didn't buy any oil; we'd just get used oil. I think we scored pistons or something. We left it in Chicago all steaming and smoking. My dad took the car. I think that's what he drove to Texas.

I never had any real financial problems up there.

Q: How were your grades in that school?

Mr. Reagan: My grades were good. I had a problem with chemistry, because my chemistry classes interfered with football practice to some extent. First year I think I was okay, and the second year we went to quantitative analysis; the classes were late. I gave up chemistry; in fact, I gave up the whole premed program, as such, and started to major in economics and sociology. Then later the war came along anyway, so it didn't seem to matter much what I did or did not take.

Q: We haven't talked about the most important aspect of your life during high school and college, and that's girls. How were you doing in that score?

Mr. Reagan: Oh, I did fine, did fine. Had a girlfriend in Montana; had a girlfriend almost everywhere, you know, at least one. Of course, I had problems in Chicago, because at one time I'd have maybe one or two or three, and one or the other of us was taking it more seriously than the other. Maybe that was the reason why I wanted to get out of Chicago.

I had a very nice girl from a very nice family up in Montana, went to school up there. And certainly had nice friendships and relationships in high school. One young lady I thought that I was going to marry. When I went away, she started going around with a guy that I didn't like too much. So I came home that winter. I forced her to say one or the other, so she said the other. Then she later wrote me, said she didn't mean it. She just did it because I forced her, but in any case, that ended that type of thing, but we became very dear friends. And then I

J. W. Reagan #2 - 143

became very friendly with a girl that I had been ignoring a bit.

Q: These things get awfully complicated.

Mr. Reagan: Yes, yes. I'd go from one thing to another. While I was down at Hampton, I met the young lady that became my first wife, my natural children's mother. We were married in September 1943, and we're very good friends, even though we've been divorced for some time. She's in Los Angeles.

My lawyer daughter Bernada just got married to another lawyer named James Head. She's up north now in Oakland. Her husband also practices law there. So she's doing okay. The other two girls, Katherine Anne and Penny Elizabeth, are in the Los Angeles area. Kathy works for the county of Los Angeles as an accounting clerk.

Q: What was your first wife's name?

Mr. Reagan: We called her "Tommie." Her maiden name was Lillian Davis.

Q: How did you meet her?

Mr. Reagan: She was in nursing school at Hampton. How I

met her, specifically, I'm not quite sure. I know I saw her; I wanted to meet her, because she was a nice-looking lady and a very nice, nice person. I'm not exactly certain how I got that arranged to meet her. But we did.

And then Sublett and I were kind of the outstanding guys in the battalion. From that point of view, I guess we had kind of an advantage, at least being known, because we were always assembling the troops to go to chow, doing the exercises, the drills, and all that sort of thing.

Q: Well, she's evidently survived her tuberculosis problem she had early in your marriage.

Mr. Reagan: Yes, she did. She gave birth to four healthy, wonderful children and did a fine job of raising them while having a full career in the nursing profession.

Q: How long did you stay with her?

Mr. Reagan: Seventeen years. I am gratified to say that we are very good friends for a long time now.

Q: So you got married, I guess, just a little before Sublett did. You guys have got so many parallels.

Mr. Reagan: Honest to God, we have. I should remember

that.

Q: He got married about the time you were commissioned, I think.

Mr. Reagan: That's right. Lillian and I were at his wedding and reception.

We do have a lot of similarities. Of course, I had another marriage in between that and this too.

Q: Well, he's had three wives also.

Mr. Reagan: Is this his third? I didn't realize that. I guess I did not know his second wife, because it was a lot of years before we got back together as a group. The only person I saw was Dennis Nelson. I saw Dennis; I saw Baugh a time or two, and I think that's about it. We didn't see each other for over 30 years, so I didn't know his second wife.

Q: I'd be interested in your more detailed memories on both of those two--Nelson and Baugh.

Mr. Reagan: I was very close friends with both of them. When I was stationed in New York, Dennis used to come down from Washington, and we'd spend a lot of time together, maybe two or three days at a time. We'd go out and go to nightclubs and have fun and sit and talk quite a bit about his career.

Q: Do you remember some of the things he used to do while you were in training at Great Lakes to be officers?

Mr. Reagan: Dennis has always had an automobile, and I guess everybody remembers him with his automobiles. He used to joke about he would be running around the base, and the shore patrol or somebody else would stop him and tell him he was going too fast. He had to slow down to 15 miles an hour or something. He said, "My car won't go that slow."

I remember him telling a joke. He said when we first got our uniforms as officers, he went down to the Palmer House and was having a dinner with all the trimmings.* He pulled out a cigar, and this dowager lady was sitting over at the table next to him and he said, "Excuse me, lady, do you mind if I smoke?"

And she said, "I don't give a damn if you burn." He had a story for everything.

Q: Well, I hope you can remember some more of them.

---
*Palmer House--a posh hotel in Chicago.

J. W. Reagan #2 - 147

Mr. Reagan: So, oh, God, I mean, he could keep them coming and going just like that.

I've stayed at his home when the Navy called me down to Washington for recruiting duty in 1949. It was because of him that I came back on active duty for the year, and then the Korean War came up. We had an annual trek going around to schools, trying to encourage young, black, qualified people to become interested in NROTC.* So I would go down to his place in Washington and we'd talk about where we'd gone, and things of that type.

Q: Was he a man to have grandiose dreams?

Mr. Reagan: I'm not so certain of that about Dennis. To look at him and the image that he projected, you would think so, but I think underneath that he was pretty much business and very serious. He was very, very free to do whatever he wanted to, because his wife Evangeline never tied him down. He was a very, very good father, very good husband in terms of supporting his family and seeing that they had what they needed and everything. But he was always off and running, you know, and he had a lot of friends--men and women friends. But underneath it all, I

---

*NROTC--Naval Reserve Officer Training Corps, a program through which students receive training to become naval officers at the same time they are attending college or university. The Navy subsidizes all or part of the cost of an individual's education under this program.

think he was a very, very serious and practical man.

Q: Well, it sounds like he really had two different personalities.

Mr. Reagan: I guess you could say that he did, and I guess he handled them both pretty well. He had a career with the Navy, and then he had a career with the National Urban League, then he had a career with the Small Business Administration.

Incidentally, did you get to talk with Evangeline?

Q: I did, yes.*

Mr. Reagan: See, he had his sons start Navy careers. I'm not quite sure where they finished.

Q: I got the impression from somebody that he pushed them a great deal in that regard, and maybe they resented that.

Mr. Reagan: It wouldn't surprise me.

When Dennis bought his home out here in Point Loma, it wasn't popular.** It wasn't a popular move at all, and he

---
*Evangeline Nelson, Dennis Nelson's widow, has been interviewed as part of the Naval Institute's oral history program.
**Following his retirement from active duty, Dennis Nelson and his family bought a home near the Naval Training Station in San Diego.

couldn't get financing. Many neighborhoods were all white, and deeds had restrictive covenants aimed at keeping Negroes, Jewish people, and other minorities out. Realtors, financial institutions, and even state and local governments honored restrictive patterns in communities. Point Loma did not want a Negro there. But Dennis was a fighter. He finally went back to Washington and was successful in arranging the financing there and stuck out the community hostility. They finally became one of its most loved and respected families.

Q: He was not a person who was inclined to take no for an answer.

Mr. Reagan: That's right, and I liked Dennis very much. His brashness and his apparent cockiness turned a lot of people off, even people that were maybe a little close to him, and maybe who did not appreciate him at that time but do now. But I always, always took Dennis for what he was, and so we never had any problem. His style was fine; that was his style.

Q: Well, I think it's fair to say that Admiral Gravely was able to walk through some doors that Dennis Nelson had kicked open.

Mr. Reagan: That's right. Yes, that's right. Sam would be the first to say so. Dennis did kick doors. And thank goodness he got us back together in 1977, because that was all his doing. To do some of the things that he did, he had to fight a little bit.

Q: Was he the guy that came up with the nickname "Golden Thirteen?"

Mr. Reagan: I don't recall that Dennis is the one that initiated that. I can't be totally certain. What do some of the other guys recall?

Q: I haven't really been able to track it down.

Mr. Reagan: The first time I saw it, I resented the fact that somebody wrote about it being a self-proclaimed title. How we became known as the Golden Thirteen exactly, I really did not know. It was either somebody in the recruiting command when we first started getting together, or one of the PR guys before we went on the trip on the Kidd. Because we had a couple of really gung-ho young guys that were assigned to work with the reunion at sea.

Q: I think it's a distinctive name.

J. W. Reagan #2 - 151

Mr. Reagan: It's sticking anyway.

Q: Hair's got it on his license plate.

Mr. Reagan: Yes, that's what I understand.

I guess Jim is so happy that--and we're all very happy, too, that everybody got together with him.

Q: He's got so much enthusiasm for it.

Mr. Reagan: Yes.

Dennis has been kind of a part of my life off and on. Every once in a while he would come by. Dennis introduced me to the second wife.

Q: Who was she?

Mr. Reagan: She was a physician, Hazel P. Morse, before we were married. I'm not certain how Dennis knew Hazel, but I know once we were in Los Angeles one day and it was very hot. He said, "Come on, I've got a friend. Come by, and we'll go swimming in her pool." We went out, and we went swimming in her pool. I think she was at her office, but probably came before we left. When I was home the next afternoon, her nurse called me and said I left my wallet over at the poolside. Then we struck up a friendship.

J. W. Reagan #2 - 152

When some things started going a little awry with the first one, I started a relationship with Hazel. We were together close to 20 years between 1960 and 1980.

Q: Well, do you have any more on Baugh that you remember?

Mr. Reagan: I did get to see Dalton, because when I went back in the Navy, I had a trip on down the eastern seaboard there. And I know Dalton was in Boston. His first wife was still alive, and the boys were just kids. Dalton was, I think at this time, in research at MIT. But even before that we were buddy-buddies. I mean, we went out together and had our drinks and our talks, and we were just buddies, just buddies. I think Dalton was the kind of guy that you could talk to in the most secret type things. So we were just very close, and I suppose you feel like that with several guys, but Dalton and Dennis, I would say--during those times we were close. And Gravely and I were pretty close over here at the section base in San Diego. We played ball together and were just close friend types.

Q: What kind of personality would you say Baugh had?

Mr. Reagan: I would say that Dalton was a pretty outgoing guy, especially at those earlier times. He had a good sense of humor. He wasn't the extrovert that Dennis was.

Q: Few people are.

Mr. Reagan: Yes, I know. That's true, that's true. With Dennis, you know, they broke the mold. But Dalton had a very, very fine personality; I mean, he could get along with anybody. I would say he was very smooth. When we got back together after many years, he seemed to be a bit more serious. Of course, he had his business and everything to run. But I think he was just a wonderful person, one that you could have as a confidant, and you could go to him for advice. He was very level-headed and just a wonderful guy to be able to call a friend.

Q: You mentioned in the first interview that before you went into the Navy you had some ROTC experience. What was involved in that?

Mr. Reagan: Oh, at Montana State I went out for ROTC. I must have joined at the start of the fall semester in 1941, so I really had only a short period in the ROTC, and then the war came along and I left school to go into the Air Force.

Q: Was the ROTC compulsory?

J. W. Reagan #2 - 154

Mr. Reagan: I don't believe it was compulsory, but I'm not completely sure.

Q: What got you into it then?

Mr. Reagan: I'm not sure, except that I think I liked the way the fellows looked when they got all dressed up. They looked like such a gung-ho bunch. I thought I would just like to go ahead and be involved in it. I'm not sure of any other reason.

Q: Was that an integrated unit?

Mr. Reagan: My freshman year there was Joe Taylor, Paul Billings, and I. There was also a young lady that didn't have much to do with any blacks--but I understand that she was black--and one other fellow. I think five blacks were the most that were in the school at that time. Maybe three of us were there in the ROTC unit.

Q: Was ROTC useful background for you when you went into the Navy?

Mr. Reagan: I think so. It got me at least on speaking terms with some military terms and marching and cadence calling and all of that. I think we took our rifles apart and things of that type, basic military stuff. So boot camp was not that awesome a thing.

Q: We haven't talked much about your boot camp. What are your memories of that?

Mr. Reagan: I'm not sure how this happened, but I remember being selected the apprentice CPO, apprentice chief petty officer. Then we had the company clerk and all of this. I took it seriously, and I ran the company. The chief wasn't around, and he started coming around less and less. I don't know whether he was watching me some place or not, but the company was doing everything it was supposed to do. I got it ready for inspections; got people out to go to chow; supervised the whole routine. Together we just kind of ran it.

Q: That calls for a fair amount of organizational ability, to get people where they need to be on time and so forth.

Mr. Reagan: Yes, but it was fairly simple because it was all set out. I just had to see that everything was done.

Q: Did you have people in the company who had problems with reading or with cleanliness and that sort of thing?

J. W. Reagan #2 - 156

Mr. Reagan: Well, if we did we got that taken care of, too, because we were always in good shape--shipshape. As far as cleanliness, I used to steel wool the barracks and polish things. The one problem I remember is a guy wetting the bed. We tried to scare him out of that. We put a lot of pressure on him. I think he got worse wetting his hammock. Then, all of a sudden, it seemed that he got better and stopped doing it. But that was the one thing that I remember mostly.

I don't remember any problems coming up that we couldn't handle. I think we had a couple of guys that wanted to be a little different, a little tough, or something like that. We somehow got everybody into shape, and I think we had a very good company.

Q: What do you remember about the curriculum in boot camp?

Mr. Reagan: Oh, I don't remember anything remarkable about it, to tell you the truth. I guess we had The Bluejackets' Manual and we studied that, and I don't remember personally having any problems with those sort of things.* I suppose we had classes and groups and things like that that we helped each other out on. I don't remember anything too

---

*The Bluejackets' Manual, which has now been published in 20 editions since the beginning of the century, is a basic handbook for enlisted personnel in a wide range of Navy subjects, including such things as ship nomenclature, signaling, manual of arms, and seamanship.

J. W. Reagan #2 - 157

remarkable about it, though. There were some guys that had a little more education than others.

Q: Well, I would think that would give you an advantage in that leadership role.

Mr. Reagan: Yes, I had some college, and there were a lot of other guys in the company, too, that had had some schooling. I'm not quite sure whether anybody had degrees.

Q: Is there any special knack to sleeping in a hammock?

Mr. Reagan: I think probably a little getting used to it first, but I think after you're in it the first couple of days, there's nothing to it. You feel right at home in it. You can hang your feet over the side without turning over.

Q: What do you recall about the practical aspects of boot camp--getting out on the rifle range or obstacle course, and that sort of thing?

Mr. Reagan: I loved the physical training; I loved that obstacle course. I think the physical training side of it was very, very important to me, because I was still at that time great on keeping in shape. We weren't in organized sports, football and things like that, but we certainly

J. W. Reagan #2 - 158

played informally.

Q: Graham Martin said he used to run the obstacle course several times a day just for fun.

Mr. Reagan: I felt like that. I'd never get tired of anything at that time. I just enjoyed this whole boot camp experience.

Q: Did you get over a sense of disappointment about not going into the Air Force?

Mr. Reagan: Not easily. I just could not see why they could not let me out of the Navy when I'd only been in there about a week when I got my orders to report to the Air Force. I was disappointed, and probably it lingered, because I was wondering about how it would have been to be involved with the Air Force. Then, after I'd been in a couple of years--this was a little bit after we got our commissions, I was around the Theresa Hotel in New York. There I saw some of the guys that had been in the 99th Pursuit Squadron, some of the guys that had been in action and had been shot down.* I saw some who had one leg or something like that, and I discovered that a lot of the

---
*The 99th Pursuit Squadron (later 99th Fighter Squadron) comprised black pilots trained at Tuskegee, Alabama. The squadron was in action in the North African and European theaters during World War II. Of the approximately 300 Tuskegee fighter pilots who went overseas, 66 were killed in action, 10 killed in accidents, and 32 taken as prisoners of war and later repatriated.

guys were lost. So I thought, "Well, maybe it was for the best."

Q: You never know what was down that road you didn't take.

Mr. Reagan: It's very true. It seems that a lot of the things you thought you wanted to do didn't happen; you don't know why it didn't happen. For instance, I thought I'd get in the Navy, I'd go through boot camp, and I'd go right aboard a ship. We'd go sailing around on a ship--battles or ports and different things like that. But it didn't happen that way.

I think about my kid too. We got him in the Navy on a minority enlistment.* Lillian and I were separated, but we both still signed for him. The minute his minority enlistment was over, he went into the Marines. He got in that situation, and he was back and forth. I did get to see him on his last leave, and he was really nervous because he said, "You just don't know. You're around people in the daytime that you think they're your friends," thinking about the Vietnamese people. "And then at night, they're with the Cong, and so you just never know who really is your friend."

---
*A minority enlistment begins before an individual's 18th birthday and ends just before his 21st birthday. That is, he serves his enlistment while still a minor. Enlistment prior to the age of 18 requires parental consent.

Q: What motivated him to go into the Marine Corps?

Mr. Reagan: I don't know why he went in the Marine Corps. I used to feel so guilty when I'd think he just wanted to show me what a man he was. Maybe he did think so, that it was a tougher service, and he wanted to be gung-ho or something like that. I really don't know.

And, of course, I think back on my own family. The separation's a little tough on the kids. I'm sure that it was kind of tough on Skip, and kids at times tend to place blame on the one that they're with for the other one being away. I think there may have been a little of that, although I know that he became very manly in the family and protective of my former wife and the girls. They looked up to him.

So I'm not totally certain why Skip made that change. I was very unhappy when he was killed.

Q: How old was he then?

Mr. Reagan: Probably 23.

Q: I can understand why that would be a real blow to you.

Mr. Reagan: Oh, God. You think, "There goes that."

Q: Well, especially because you'd planned to go into business with him.

Mr. Reagan: My only son. That was the first one, first and only. I could say, "That's the end of the Reagans." That's what I'm thinking, but, of course, there's my brother. His sons are in Norway and in Denmark. But they're Reagans.

So, yes, it was quite a bad spell for me for a time.

Q: You mentioning the Air Force, there's another intriguing parallel with Sublett, because he also tried to get into the Air Force.

Mr. Reagan: I didn't know that. The more I know about Sublett, the more I think that some things about us parallel.

Q: Oh, indeed. In fact, he had been playing football, and he had to get down to a certain weight to get into the Air Force. He made the effort, and then they didn't have an opening for him.

Mr. Reagan: Isn't that amazing. If I knew, I didn't recall that.

Q: Did your company or you, as an individual, win any honors out of boot camp?

Mr. Reagan: I believe we did. I don't remember the incident as such, but I remember some pictures somebody had where we were holding a flag that was related to some kind of honor. We had a hell of a marching unit, because the little kid that did the drilling for my company had been to college at one of the southern schools, and he would have been involved in the band, in the marching team. He really had us marching. I'm just certain that we won some kind of honors there, but I can't recall the exact things. When they had the dedication of this building, it brought back a lot of that stuff to me, companies marching in review and everything.* But enough time has passed so I just don't recall what the specific deals were. But I know we were a top company in the regiment.

Q: And then you went from there to Hampton, I guess.

Mr. Reagan: Right.

Q: Did they generally pick the top men out of boot camp to

---

*On 6 June 1987, the in-processing building for recruits at the Great Lakes Naval Training Center was named in honor of the Golden Thirteen.

go to service school?

Mr. Reagan: Well, my understanding was that they based service school selections on the classification test. Now, why they would pick me for electrical school, I don't know.

Q: Did you have any experience in that regard?

Mr. Reagan: Had no experience as an electrician.

I guess maybe the scores were good enough in those classification tests that they said, "Well, this guy should be able to make it in electrical school." I don't think there was a preference thing to it, as I recall, whether you could name the school that you went to.

Q: Was the electrical knowledge something you picked up pretty readily at Hampton?

Mr. Reagan: Yes, and I think I was a pretty good electrician's mate. The first job I had was in the battery locker down here at the sea frontier base at Point Loma. And then aboard the <u>Firefly</u>, an auxiliary minesweep, in the summer of 1943.

We had a couple of jobs to do on that. The gear wasn't working right. We had to pull it out and find out what was wrong with it, generating equipment and things like that. And then I just studied and took the test for second class petty officer a year later. I didn't think my experience had been that great, but I took it and passed it. I didn't get any tougher duties than going out and sweeping. But then it wasn't too long after that that I was transferred to Norfolk aboard a DE, and Downes saw me over there, and he sent me back up to Great Lakes for officer training.

Q: What do you remember about the level of instruction there in service school?

Mr. Reagan: Very good.

We had an instructor that formerly taught at Prairie View.* He was just excellent in teaching the theory, and I really enjoyed his class.

Q: How much of the military side of it was there in the school? You said that you and Sublett were leaders there.

Mr. Reagan: We had regular drills of the battalion. And then the various platoons at their will, I guess, would go out and practice sometimes. We had competitions between the companies. And, of course, we had the battalion review every Saturday. We had quite a bit of military drill, I

---
*Prairie View A&M, a black college in Prairie View, Texas.

would say.

   We didn't do an awful lot of weapons training and things of that type, because our greatest involvement was in our classes. The school had electrical, motor machinist's mate, and carpentry classes.

Q: Metalsmith.

Mr. Reagan: Metalsmith, yes. And I think the level of instruction was very high, very high.

Q: What qualities do you remember about Commander Downes?

Mr. Reagan: I thought he was the epitome of a military officer. I thought he was a real leader. I think my image of leadership was developed primarily from him, that you didn't have to be loud, you didn't have to be this, you didn't have to be that.

Q: Didn't have to be a screamer.

Mr. Reagan: No. Because he was very calm, but very firm. He just seemed like a wonderful man to be around, but you knew he was the commanding officer, and I admired that about him. I admired his style and his manner. He was always immaculate, and looked like he could make a decision about anything. Nothing bothered him. He just looked and acted like a leader to me, the way he would handle his staff and delegate, things like that. I was very much impressed with Downes.

Q: He seemed to have a genuine concern for the students as humans.

Mr. Reagan: Oh, yes, yes. Very intelligent man. I may have said before, I think he knew everybody's name in the whole battalion.

Q: I did a little research on him, and he had a master's degree in education from Columbia. So he was very well suited to that environment.

Mr. Reagan: Yes, he was right at home. Right at home. And I think he did a lot for that school too.

Q: Do you remember any specific incidents involving Commander Downes?

Mr. Reagan: I think we got a boat around there at some point, and he asked Sublett and me to take him for a ride. I just seem to remember him sitting there, enjoying the ride. He was a tremendous conversationalist, and he just kept chatter going. I don't remember any incident involving the officers, his staff, or us, except that I think the morale was very high, and I think that it was because of him a great deal. Of course, most of the people there were pretty highly motivated, I believe. I don't remember anything that I can say of specific nature for Downes.

At one point, he had me back over in his quarters to half explain to me why I wasn't going aboard the DE. He couldn't come right out and say I was going to officer training.

I think I've seen him angry about something maybe once or twice. When I say anger for him, I mean he was not polite. I can't think what it was. I don't know if he was bawling some staff person out because this individual had said something that could be taken as racial, because Commander Downes was death on that. But that could well have been one of the things that I would remember. Or he wouldn't be averse probably to taking down one of us if we had done something that we should not have.

I don't recall anybody getting into any serious trouble from the battalion over there, but with the number of people, it wouldn't surprise me that he had seen somebody at captain's mast or something. We tried to self-police ourselves to a great extent, but there's always somebody that may get a little bit out of line.

Q: You're also talking about a pretty high caliber of student there.

Mr. Reagan: I really think so. As I look back on it, I think we had a hell of a group.

Q: Sublett said that on liberty he stuck pretty much there to the base. Was that your experience, also?

Mr. Reagan: Pretty much, although Lillian was living out in town. I would visit her, and we would go to movies and spend quite a bit of time together off campus.

I'm not quite sure of Sublett's relationships at the school. His first wife was from Chicago.

Q: Well, he said generally there was not a very hospitable climate for blacks outside the gate at Hampton, so he avoided that situation.

Mr. Reagan: I know that if you went to the movie, you had to sit in the balcony, things like that.

I don't remember staying, unless there was something going on in the campus, maybe something in the auditorium. I do remember at one time Marian Anderson came to the college itself, and we, of course, attended.* In fact, I had to take her a bouquet. I remember looking at her red shoes, and I think I knocked the vase over, but I didn't get her feet wet.

Q: Was there much interaction between the students at the college and the Navy men?

Mr. Reagan: Yes, and I think it was very healthy, very good. I don't know how the guys on the campus looked at us, because I think the sailors took a lot of the girls.

Q: You described before a confrontation you had with the bus driver. How was that eventually resolved?

Mr. Reagan: Oh, well, the lady driver said she was not going to move. Finally, there was also one young guy there who said, "Let the guy stay on. The bus is crowded back there."

She said, "I'm not moving."

So finally one of the city cops, I believe, came around and said, "Well, you'll have to get off the bus." I still just stood there, as I recall, for a while. Then he

---

*Marian Anderson was a concert contralto, famous for singing at the Lincoln Memorial in the late 1930s after being denied permission to sing at the hall of the Daughters of the American Revolution. She was among the best-known black Americans of the period.

said, "Well, come on, son, you've got to get off. That's the law."

So I sat there a little while trying to be stubborn. I said, "I'm not getting off until she gives me my dime back." So she gave me my dime back, and I got off. I don't recall whether I still went into town or not or found a less crowded bus and got on or whether I went back to the barracks. That was the way that ended.

Q: That would kill your enthusiasm for liberty.

Mr. Reagan: I think it did that time.

I'm sure that Lillian, my future wife, wasn't at Hampton then, so I had no reason to go just to get off the base. I probably just went back on the base.

Q: We talked not at all about your experiences out in California before you went back for officer training. What do you remember about that period?

Mr. Reagan: Well, of course, when I was here I had no inkling of what was ahead. I was stationed down at Point Loma, and, of course, Lillian was out here. I was liberty-bound every weekend and during the week as well. My job was in the battery locker at the base or on the _Firefly_, the auxiliary sweep that we had. We'd go out with the guys

J. W. Reagan #2 - 171

and go down to the Douglas Hotel and have a few beers and tell sea stories. On weekends I usually took three or four guys up with me because my mother was living in Los Angeles. Everybody knew her as "Mother Dear," so she had a little family of sailors.

Late fall of '43 was when I got orders to go down to Norfolk, to go aboard this DE. So time seemed to have kind of gone pretty much. Mostly it was family here on liberties and weekends. And then doing a job, go off doing the sweeping, whatever we had to do.

Then also, Sam Gravely and I were involved with softball quite a bit. So we had a game of softball every once in a while. Sam used to run the pool hall, and then he got to be kind of friendly with the athletic officer on the section base down there. So we played on the softball team together. I'd go down, when I had nothing else to do, and shoot pool in this pool hall.

Q: What were the shipboard duties like?

Mr. Reagan: I enjoyed them immensely. We would go out beyond the gates and sweep all day.

Q: Real mines, or what?

Mr. Reagan: We were looking for mines, yes. I don't think

J. W. Reagan #2 - 172

we ever brought any up. It seems like one time we did shoot at one. We might have gotten ahold of one once. It's dim recollection. It looks like we were shooting at one to explode it.

Q: Was the crew all black?

Mr. Reagan: No, no, it was mixed. I'm trying to think how many of us. There were probably two or three white guys on this particular crew of seven. It was a converted fishing vessel with the sweep gear.

I remember it used to get kind of rough sometimes right outside the breakwater. The worst thing I remember about that is that I got a hell of an appetite when it was rolling, and nobody wanted to eat. You know, we were eating the horse stuff, because it was too rough to eat.*

But most of the time we were just letting the gear out and watching the gear. Occasionally, a generator would break down, or something else would happen with some of the electrical gear. You'd find a short somewhere, or something like that, and fix it. Most of the time it would be checking the volt meter to see that the output was okay. But then sometimes it was so nice and calm, you'd just go out and look down at the water. You could see down to the

---

*Mr. Reagan has here used a euphemism for the Navy slang term "horse cock," which is used to refer to cold cuts sliced from a long roll of meat.

bottom in some places.

All in all, it was a pleasant duty. We were aware that the antisubmarine nets were important there, and so we didn't want to damage them. Sweeping the harbor area was a duty that needed to be done during wartime. But I would say, basically, that that duty aboard the Firefly was a fairly enjoyable duty.

Q: What made it enjoyable?

Mr. Reagan: Well, I just like the water for one thing. I like to be out moving on the water and looking at the ocean. I just enjoyed being aboard a ship or boat, anything. It's a wonder I don't have one.

Q: It's unfortunate the Navy didn't give you more of an opportunity in that regard.

Mr. Reagan: Yes, it is. I think I expected that we would go aboard ships. But I can understand now that there are jobs and there are jobs, and we were at the time considered experimental by the higher-ups. That's my opinion. I never thought myself as just being a reserve officer. I was an officer, and I know that in regular peacetime Navy, there were certain things you do. You'd probably get to be a junior officer in a division or department, and go on

J. W. Reagan #2 - 174

that route. But I think for a lot of it, what they did with us was more or less a pattern, and I think they were just, maybe, trying to get us adjusted to the general duty services, and getting the general Navy used to us. Of course, there were a lot of reserve officers in during that time, not just our group.

Q: Well, the comment I've heard from several of the men of the Golden Thirteen is that the Navy didn't know what to do with you.

Mr. Reagan: Didn't know what to do with us, right. So the Navy said, "Well, we'll put them in logistic support companies, or we'll put them on yard craft." Because the assignments for the group were similar throughout.

Q: Did you feel a sense of letdown as a result?

Mr. Reagan: Well, what I thought was that maybe as the war went on, that perhaps the chances of being involved more in the seagoing Navy, or whatever you want to call it, would come about. But I think the last of my second tour, in the 1950s, I enjoyed much better than my first, because I was a little disappointed to be assigned to logistics support company during World War II. The concept was, I think, good--that these companies would land and prepare for the troops that were coming in. But then there was none of that, because by the time we got over to Okinawa, the war was over.

Now in the Korean War, I was with an amphibious unit, and we had a lot of M boats.* That was a significant experience because the skipper appointed me the exec, and there were only two senior lieutenants. There was a white fellow, and everybody was thinking maybe they were going to appoint him. We got to go out, and mostly we did joint exercises.

We went out one time, I think, looking for a downed plane in the Japanese Sea. We didn't get close to it, but we located it. This other officer and I took a couple of boats out. We spotted it and called in the approximate position. I think that's about the most exciting thing we did. But, you know, things had changed a little bit by the time of Korea. I had made the senior grade lieutenant and now here was an exec. It was a fair-size outfit, mostly all Caucasian.

Q: Now you had a real job, not just training.

Mr. Reagan: Right. I had to get ready for the

---

*The M boat--commonly known as a Mike boat--is a large landing craft used for carrying such things as tanks ashore during amphibious landings. Its official designation is LCM--landing craft mechanized.

J. W. Reagan #2 - 176

administrative inspections. We had 20-some M boats that had to be up to par, everything. And you had all these junior officers that you have to relate to. Keep a lot of the paperwork off the skipper. You felt like you were involved in something. You were overseas too.

Q: By that point you had probably gotten past the feeling of being just a token.

Mr. Reagan: That's true. I felt part of the Navy--all of it.

Q: We touched fairly briefly on your experience during the officer training at Great Lakes. Do you have any recollections of Armstrong as a personality from that period?

Mr. Reagan: I think I've said this before, too, that the thing that I remember about Armstrong is that he was a very aristocratic type looking person.

Q: Was he that way in manner, also?

Mr. Reagan: I would say that he was, yes. That's just a general image that I have of him. I don't recall having any sort of close relationship with him. I'm sure Goodwin did, as I heard later, as a go-between. And I think Dennis had some--at least as I recall in Dennis's book, he was quite negative about Armstrong.

Q: Did you have that negative feeling toward him?

Mr. Reagan: I didn't. I didn't have any reason to.

Q: Did you have much contact with him?

Mr. Reagan: No, I did not. I just saw him and knew he was there and knew that he was the head of the thing. But I didn't have any feelings about Armstrong one way or the other. The relationship with Downes was the thing that I remember mostly over and above Armstrong.

Q: But I gather that was a more positive relationship than the one with Armstrong.

Mr. Reagan: Oh, yes. I don't even recall any kind of a feeling of a relationship with Armstrong at all except that he was there and we were where we were.

Q: What are your recollections of John Dille from early 1944?[*]

---

[*]Lieutenant (junior grade) John F. Dille, Jr., USNR, was a battalion officer at Camp Robert Smalls. He has been interviewed by the Naval Institute's oral history program.

Mr. Reagan: I remember Dille being involved with us, with the group, and being supportive. And I guess that I probably related to John much more in later years than at the time. I thought the class was an excellent thing, and I felt grateful to be a part of this thing. But at the time, in my inner self, I was so engrossed about being out in the Navy that it wasn't as big of a deal with me right then as it became when the class went on and we did become commissioned. There were some difficult things about the class, because some of us knew more about some things than others. As an overall thing, it didn't seem like a really difficult thing.

We were aware of the fact that we were in this big barracks and all of that. We did things together, but I think we were mostly concerned about doing well in the classes.

I remember Dille; I remember Payton.

Q: What do you recall about Payton?

Mr. Reagan: Well, I thought he was a very, very smart man. I don't know how well I knew him, but it seems to me I knew Payton at Hampton or had met him.

Q: What did he teach?

Mr. Reagan: He was strong in mathematics. And I guess that's what he taught in the OCS class.*

Q: Math per se seems like an unlikely subject.

Mr. Reagan: Yes, it does. I don't think he taught navigation. What did Payton teach? Maybe he did teach us math; I'm not sure.

Q: I would certainly like to get hold of the records for that class, if they still exist, and see.

Mr. Reagan: Yes. I should review that. What other courses that I knew--I remember navigation, gunnery . . .

Q: Navy regs.

Mr. Reagan: Navy regs, customs, seamanship--I'm trying to think what he would be teaching.

Q: Since you didn't take this as that big a deal, did you feel a sense of pressure from that environment?

Mr. Reagan: I really don't think so. I really don't think

---
*OCS--Officer Candidate School.

J. W. Reagan #2 - 180

that I did. I wanted to do well, and I studied. I don't know if I had stress mixed with pressure or not, but I don't remember it being stressful.

I really don't recall that I felt under pressure that I could identify it as such. The day was full, but I don't think we had too many problems about the subjects and, generally, we'd dig it out, or somebody would know something about something if we had questions about it or problems about it, and everybody was supportive of each other.

Q: Some of the guys have mentioned the idea that each one of your group was representing several thousand black enlisted men.

Mr. Reagan: Yes, yes.

Q: Was that a thing you talked about at the time?

Mr. Reagan: I don't recall specifically that we really got into that a lot at the time. And I don't know that we all were sure that we were going to be commissioned for one thing. From the start of being in the Navy and the general services, I think many of us thought that we should do just as well as possible, because it was a new thing. So I would be certain that as officers, or as potential officers, we would have that feeling, and we probably did discuss it. If we became officers we would be examples, and a lot of what we did might depend a lot on what the Navy did thereafter. So in that sense, I'm sure that being the kind of guys that we were and we were with, that we would have those discussions. I don't recall anything more outstanding than just being in the class and doing the class work.

Q: I got the impression that Goodwin was something of a self-appointed disciplinarian. Do you remember him in that role?

Mr. Reagan: I remember it vaguely, just Goodwin's manner and personality. I don't go so far to say that it impressed me to the point that I could feel toward Goodwin something like, "Who appointed you to be the disciplinarian?" I know some of the guys remember him in that way, but I'm not sure of that myself, because I didn't know Goodwin that well. I don't know whether he had some motives or some aspirations to be in that role or felt that it was needed.

Q: I gather it was more the latter, that he felt it was needed and a useful thing for the welfare of the group.

J. W. Reagan #2 - 182

Mr. Reagan: That might be right.

Q: And then there was Jesse Arbor for comic relief.

Mr. Reagan: No question about that. Jesse was--I mean, he was, he was Jesse. He's always been and I think he will always be. See, other than Dennis Nelson, I don't know anyone that has a story for almost anything but Jesse. He's also a very deep guy, but he has his stories, and he could lighten up a situation very quickly.

Q: Do you remember cases of getting outside the barracks to shoot guns or for rifle range or physical training?

Mr. Reagan: Well, antiaircraft practice.

Q: Where was that?

Mr. Reagan: We had gunnery practice at Great Lakes.

Q: Did they have a special setup with these guns?

Mr. Reagan: Yes, they had the plane towing this sleeve.

Q: But the guns were mounted on shore rather than ship, I gather. Is that what you're saying?

Mr. Reagan: Yes. It seems the only time that I've had experience firing shipboard weapons was on one of the two-week tours when I was in the reserves. I don't recall firing ours off a ship when we were in OCS.

Q: It's interesting to hear the reactions to the instructors. A couple of members of the Golden Thirteen remember them as condescending, and you didn't have that recollection at all. I guess to you they just seemed straightforward and interested in your progress.

Mr. Reagan: I'm trying to review and recall if I have any reason to change that impression. I don't think that I can recall that I had that feeling about the instructors. Or if I did, I may have had the feeling that that's the way they would instruct anybody. I'm sure they had some feeling, possibly, because of our being the first class of black officer candidates. But it's just not an outstanding thing in my memory of the class.

Q: Well, there again, then, your memory coincides with Sublett because he's one who doesn't remember anything of that nature.

Mr. Reagan: I didn't know how similar my and Sublett's

backgrounds were before.

Q: I think fairly similar.

Mr. Reagan: Yes. And it may have been, because of the kinds of experiences that we may have had in school settings and things like that, I don't know. I don't have those piercing, pinpointing views about people, because it just seems to me that I've seen a lot of different kinds of people. I've seen that people seem to be types regardless of what they are or what setting you define. If there's a certain type of individual in one group, you find the same kind of guy in another group.

Q: Well, the two of you had come up in essentially integrated environments, so this is not all that different from what you were used to.

Mr. Reagan: Yes, as far as different people are concerned, I always assumed that, perhaps, we might pay a little less attention to it, maybe, than some of the guys that had different experiences. I look at the guys, and I guess White's been in Chicago all of his life. I spent a lot of time in Chicago. But, you know, a lot of places in the North there was a lot of segregation, too. I think Baugh and Arbor and Hair and some of those fellows had quite a

J. W. Reagan #2 - 185

significant experience in the South, where things were not just subtly segregated. They were segregated, period.

Q: Cooper did too.

Mr. Reagan: Yes, and Cooper did. Sam Barnes was a northerner, I guess.

Q: Yes.

Mr. Reagan: An integrated college. So I don't know. You probably, based on the experience or the environment that you're in, maybe have a different attitude, different perception of things. Not good or bad, but just different.

Q: Right. What was your reaction when you found out that you had been investigated by the FBI?*

Mr. Reagan: I guess I thought, "These people are serious about this thing." I was wondering if I had done anything. I suppose I thought that this was to be expected. Again, I don't know if I related it to whether they do that to everybody or if they just did it to our group. I suppose it might have gone a little bit further

---
*The Federal Bureau of Investigation did thorough checks on the backgrounds of potential black officer candidates before they were chosen for the program.

J. W. Reagan #2 - 186

with us. It was an event for us. It was also an event for the higher-ups and the political types that knew it was coming about. So I suppose that they would be a bit more cautious or concerned about backgrounds because that could be a lot of--and I'm sure there was--a lot of political criticism and that sort of thing about it, not just ethnically. Maybe both tied together.

Q: Was it a thing that bothered you that it had been done?

Mr. Reagan: I don't think it bothered me that much, no. I don't recall it bothering me.

Q: Is there anything else about that experience at Great Lakes that sticks in your mind? That's the core experience for all of you, and I'm trying to get as much of that as I can.

Mr. Reagan: I don't know at what point I got this feeling: if you're going to have more people, you've got to have more space. But even at that time, I was wondering if that was the most efficient way to operate--on a segregated basis. I believe that I've always had this kind of concern about things. I just thought--and this may have always been a general thing with me--that a setup like Camp Robert Smalls was a wasteful way to do things. It might have been the largest scale that I've ever seen a segregated situation. I don't know. That may be the largest overall impression that I have about Great Lakes.

Also, I do know that Dennis was at one time assigned to remedial reading work, and I was somewhat surprised, and maybe a little bit depressed at the number of people who were not able to read or write and that it was necessary to have a special class for that sort of thing. I was a little depressed that out there in the general population in the United States of America that we had, perhaps, greater numbers of people that were illiterate than I had imagined that there were. That would be a kind of an outstanding thing in my mind.

Q: I hope we're better off today.

Mr. Reagan: Well, I hope so. We probably are in a relative sense, anyway.

Q: I continue to hear about literacy programs, which suggests there's still a problem to be solved.

Mr. Reagan: I don't know, but in the whole population I find kids have a hard time making out job applications. When I was with the Urban League in Pasadena, we set up those kind of training situations to teach kids how to make out applications, how to go on job interviews. We knew that New York had set up a street academy for dropouts. We started one in Pasadena, and we got quite a few kids that had dropped out of high school involved in this. And then we got a fair percentage of those back in the mainstream of education.

So many, many years after the boot camp experience, there's still a lot of things that haven't been solved yet. I guess the whole education system sometimes comes under fire in terms of such things as where we stand in terms of teaching the sciences, as opposed to what the Koreans and the Japanese are doing with their kids.

There's that general concern, and then there's the issue of poor people and poor districts and the people maybe having to try to go to work instead of going to school and things like that. So I guess it's a difference in degree, but somehow there is a huge need to find ways to assist and motivate poor and minority youth to learn the value of and to get a good education. Even though opportunity is more available, it is still a highly competitive society and one that places a premium on education.

You see promotions on TV about reading classes. A fellow comes up there and says, "Now I know how to read," and he's happy. So there's a lot of it still.

Sometimes you get in situations where you're closer to

it than others. I distinctly remember that about the Great Lakes remedial program. That's how I started learning about remedial education.

Q: What kind of sense of satisfaction did you feel when you found that you would be one of the 13 and got to put on the officer's uniform?

Mr. Reagan: I'd say it was exhilarating; it was thrilling. This hadn't happened before and it was very great. I guess, it's like you might have a dream about something, or maybe a goal. Something unusual, wonderful, and fine happens to you and you get to sit down, maybe, in a little while and say, "What does it all mean? This really has happened, hasn't it?" From that point of view, I got a terrific sense of satisfaction.

There used to be a lot about "first this" and "first that," and being the first was kind of a great thing. But maybe you had to wonder about why it's such a great thing. It represented an important step and an important personal potential that it's possible for things to happen, and they're very encouraging on a personal level, and, I guess, for others too.

Q: Well, validation of that is the fact that you were on a page of _Life_ magazine.

Mr. Reagan: Yes, it was happening, all right, and it was an event in our history. At least as we were asked to come to these things like the trip to Scotland, or they dedicated a building to us, what can you say?* We were the first group of black people commissioned in the Navy, and that's just the way that happened. You accept it and know that it was a thing that hadn't happened before, and you were fortunate enough to be a part of it.

Q: You talked about the feeling of satisfaction from getting commissioned. What was the attitude of the 13 who did toward the three who didn't?

Mr. Reagan: As I recall, we were called out one or two or three at a time--I don't know if the paperwork was coming in that way or what--for some period of time, a day or so. Then I believe that after the 13 of us had gotten our commissions, we were called over to some officer's office and were all congratulated and everything. That was the last I remember hearing of it. I don't remember seeing the three fellows by the time we got back from whatever was happening about that time: waiting for orders and different things like that.

---

*In February 1989, Reagan and the other surviving members of the Golden Thirteen were invited to travel to Scotland to visit the submarine tender Simon Lake (AS-33) as part of the ship's observance of Black History Month.

J. W. Reagan #2 - 191

I'm not sure what our response was to them not being around, whether it was just wondering what happened to the other three that were left there. I'm not sure that the officer said anything about it--"You 13 fellows are the ones that are commissioned and . . ." I don't remember them saying anything about the three guys that weren't. I feel certain that we wondered about it, and wondered what happened with the guys.

It may have been at that time that someone said, "Well, I think that Alves, something was wrong with his application because he had at one time put that his ethnic background was Portuguese," or something like that. Pinkney, I don't know. I believe it was something about education, that it was misstated or something on the application. Some things like that.

Q: Where did you hear these things about Alves and Pinkney?

Mr. Reagan: It seems to me it was right about the time, right after they were not involved. Now it could have been, if they had some knowledge of this, they might have said it to somebody, one or more of the other guys in the group, and the guys brought it out at that time. I'm not just quite certain as to how that came about. But I do remember a curiosity about what happened to the other three guys and why they didn't make it. And I think there were these kinds of discussions or whether they were just rumors or whether these guys had confided in one or the other people that they knew in the group, that they thought that they might not make it because of this sort of thing.

Q: Were you disappointed that you got sent back to Hampton rather than to sea duty?

Mr. Reagan: Yes, I was disappointed, and I was curious as to why I would be going back there and I would become the electrical officer, rather than going out someplace and going aboard ship. Then I thought, "Well, maybe this is just an interim type thing," and it turned out to be. Sublett and Cooper and I went back down to Hampton.

Q: Was your job as an officer at Hampton substantially different when you went back from what it had been before?

Mr. Reagan: Yes, because, of course, we were enlisted trainees in the service school before. In 1944, I was made the officer in charge of the electrical school. For whatever that meant, I would show up there and try to give a little pep talk or something to the students and ask the instructor how they were doing and how they were coming along, and that sort of thing. It was not a substantive type of activity. Then we'd go out on the boat and fool around, Sublett and I. It seems that we were just there waiting for something.

Q: Well, one thing you were able to do was to be an example of what these black enlisted men could aspire to.

Mr. Reagan: Well, that could be part of it too.

Q: How did your relationship with Downes change when you were an officer? Did you have more contact with him then?

Mr. Reagan: It was a little more social. We'd have lunch with him and things of that type, and I believe that's about the extent of it. I don't remember that I related to him that much more closely. Cooper probably had as much contact with him, or maybe more.

Q: Apparently so.

Mr. Reagan: I guess Cooper stayed there after we left. I'm not sure.

Q: He did. He stayed there the rest of the time in the Navy, and then he got out on a physical discharge.

Mr. Reagan: Well, yes, you sent me a copy of Cooper's interview. Of course, I hadn't realized that he'd gotten out on a physical disability.

Q: What do you remember about your time in the YTB with Hair?

Mr. Reagan: Well, I remember we had a lot of good times. We had a good cook aboard, had a lot of fun switching on and off. I guess the biggest thing I remember about the YTB was a kind of tragic event. One time when Hair wasn't aboard, we were helping a loaded-down LST get away from the docks down at, I guess it was Bayonne, ammunition pier. We were on the starboard side, and the pilot instructed us to let loose and go around to the port side and help him out because the current was heavier than we thought. And in doing so, we got tipped and lost a couple of people. That was the worst thing that personally has ever happened with me in the Navy, to lose the people.

Q: Was there an investigation afterward?

Mr. Reagan: There was an investigation. I got a letter of reprimand. I haven't seen it in the record anywhere, but I guess it's there.

It seemed like such an urgent order, and I thought about it and said, "Well, if we let loose and let it go ahead a little bit, maybe it would be going ahead too much." I understood it was to come around and give enough leeway and cut across the bow and come up on the port end of it. It wasn't a great big tip, but it was big enough that three guys went in the water, and we got one out.

Q: They didn't have life jackets on?

Mr. Reagan: Well, no, I don't recall that they did. They should have all had them on, I'm certain.

But that was a really down, down, down experience. Of course, all the other things kind of paled as far as my experience with the YTB was concerned. We were there for two or three months, I guess, when they started sending us on these logistic support company things.

Q: Did you get the same sense of enjoyment from being out on the water in that, that you had from the minesweeper?

Mr. Reagan: Oh, yes. We had some harrowing times there in that New York Harbor because of the fog and things that we were called out--somebody was in trouble way outside of the port. But then we had some nice assignments too. We did icebreaking up the Hudson; we did a lot of different things. I think we were involved with the Queen Mary at one time and some assignment there.*

Q: I'd be interested in as many of these as you remember.

Mr. Reagan: It was a nice tug, new YTB, diesel-electric, handled well. Those are the kinds of things that I remember. I guess Jim Hair had some experiences when I wasn't aboard. I've heard about he had to threaten this older chief once. They'd gone in to help fight a fire, and the chief was kind of pleading for Jim not to go. The way it got to me, Jim was about to pull out his .45 to have him get out of his way, to go out and go and help with this fire, at, on, or near an ammunition situation.

Q: Hair's a plucky little guy.

Mr. Reagan: Oh, boy, he is. He was all business on that boat.

Q: He apparently really enjoyed that, got a lot of satisfaction from it.

Mr. Reagan: No question about it, and he was a tremendous

---
*The Queen Mary was a 1,109-foot-long, 81,235-ton British passenger ship of the Cunard Line; she was converted for use as a troop transport during World War II.

sailor and ship handler. I know that I'd call on him in a minute. Sometimes I'd be on watch when we were out there in the fog, and I'd say, "Jim, come up here and make sure where we're supposed to be." He'd get up there, and it was nice to have him with you there. Jim was a great, great little guy, I'll tell you.

Q: Did you get to be a pretty good ship handler yourself?

Mr. Reagan: I got to be pretty good at it, yes. When I went back in with the M-boats, with the amphibious unit during the Korean War, it wasn't new to me. Although they had their own crews, we'd take over, and we'd go out looking for the planes and things like that. I felt pretty comfortable with it.

Before we went on the tug, I was officer in charge under instruction on a PC. And I had a little episode there one time. I said, "Oh, I'm going to have a realistic man-overboard drill." I'm going to be the one overboard, I told myself. And I told the helmsman, and I believe that's all I told. Then I dived in. We were several miles off Coney Island, and we had a pretty good current coming down. I jumped in the water, and somebody yelled, "Man overboard!" Then they all yelled, "Man overboard!" and they all came around to the side of the ship and, "Look, there's Mr. Reagan down there."

I said, "Get me a life ring! Get me up!" They did it pretty fast, but the current was coming down, and I was going toward the ship, and I wasn't getting there very fast. But they got over there and got me out. And I raised hell. I said, "You guys were standing there looking at me instead of throwing me something."

As for the antisubmarine work, if you got something on the radio about a sub approaching, you had this regular triangular thing that you would make, and we had a couple of those, but nothing ever really happened.

Q: How long were you in the PC?

Mr. Reagan: About a couple of months. Then the tug duty came up, and I was transferred over there with Jim.

Q: That would sound like a step down from a PC.

Mr. Reagan: It was.

Q: Especially if you were in command.

Mr. Reagan: Well, officer in charge under instruction.

I suppose it was, except that the tug was bigger, of course, and it was newer. You talk about a patrol craft, you know. I guess glamour-wise the PC seems a little better than a tugboat, and I suppose operational-wise too.

Q: Where did you have berthing arrangements on the tug? Did they have separate officers' quarters?

Mr. Reagan: I think in ordinary times they probably have a chief, maybe a warrant, running those things. But there was a little compartment for the officers there, little head and shower. Yes, it was different from the crew.

Q: How large a crew did you have on the tug?

Mr. Reagan: I'm thinking that we had probably under 20, with more or less two shifts split up.

Q: Were they all black?

Mr. Reagan: No, we had a white chief petty officer and a couple of white petty officers, but primarily black.

Q: Was there any friction between the groups?

Mr. Reagan: No.

Q: You probably wouldn't have permitted it to last long if it did come up.

Mr. Reagan: No, no, really. It was good morale, good crew.

Q: What led then to your assignment overseas?

Mr. Reagan: Well, I think it was along about the time that most of the guys were going with the logistic support companies. I guess this was the time that Jim Hair got sent off to the Mason.

Q: Right.

Mr. Reagan: Frank Sublett and Graham Martin had an oiler out here in San Francisco.

Q: Then they went to Eniwetok.

Mr. Reagan: Yes, we all went to different places.

Q: And Nelson was there on Eniwetok with them also.

Mr. Reagan: Yes, Dennis went out there.

Q: Arbor and Lear both went out to the Pacific.

J. W. Reagan #2 - 201

Mr. Reagan: Yes. I cannot remember whether I went first to Guam or first to Okinawa and then to Guam. And I was in charge of this one company, just to be with it until they were discharged. I went one place and then came back to the other, and then I was relieved of that duty. And I was under temporary assignment on the base. I guess that's when we got involved in building the cement field.

Q: Any other memories from that overseas duty? Were you accepted in officers' clubs?

Mr. Reagan: Oh, there was no problem there. Everybody seemed to be so miserable over there because of the mud and everything. It seems to me I met Arbor once in something called an officers' club. It seems like he was the only one in it, and there was one of the chaplains. That's just very vague to me where that was. I think maybe it was Guam.

Q: He was on Guam.

Mr. Reagan: Then I believe they had a little club of their own there in Guam, but I don't recall having any problem going into the regular club that they had on Okinawa.

In fact, the only official discrimination I recall was that first experience at Great Lakes, where we were

J. W. Reagan #2 - 202

supposedly not to go into the main side officers' club.

Q: Where did that word come from? Is that Armstrong?

Mr. Reagan: I understand that it was. And, you know, it was a slight and insulting, although personally I hadn't felt a great desire to go into an officers' club at the time. But just the fact that you could not was a real downer. I don't know if it was through Goodwin or through Nelson, or whatever. I think that situation straightened out pretty quick, as though there had never been any discrimination. I still don't recall if I visited the club before leaving Great Lakes.

Q: It was unfortunate that the hierarchy at Great Lakes said, in effect, "We're making you officers, but we're not going to treat you like officers."

Mr. Reagan: Yes, I think it was that kind of an attitude.

There was also an incident down at Port Hueneme, when I was an ensign, where the guy told me I couldn't be served because there were other people eating in this civilian restaurant. I called the officer of the day, and they sent the shore patrol down there and told him that they were going to put him off limits.

J. W. Reagan #2 - 203

Q: What took you to Port Hueneme?

Mr. Reagan: That's when I was getting ready to go overseas near the end of the war.

Q: I see.

Mr. Reagan: I guess those logistic support companies were under the engineers, for the most part, CEC people.*

Q: How long then did you stay overseas after the war ended?

Mr. Reagan: I think I came back the first of January in 1946, so I probably wasn't over there more than three or four months.

Q: Did you have any desire to stay in the Navy in 1946?

Mr. Reagan: I think I was kind of anxious to get out, because my wife was going to have our first child, and she was going to just about be released from the hospital with her TB. I was interested in going and having a family situation in civilian life.

---
*Port Hueneme, California, has long been a base for West Coast Mobile Construction Battalions (Seabees). These construction battalions are fun by officers of the Navy's Civil Engineer Corps.

J. W. Reagan #2 - 204

In '46 I don't think I had any real desire to stay in. Also, I had not finished school, and so I got out and I went back to New York and stayed. I worked with a boys' home for a while, and waiting for Lillian's release, which was to be three or four months off. While I was there, as I mentioned before, Doug Fessenden called me from Montana and asked me to come back and get my other year of eligibility and finish school. Skip was born in March of that year, and we had Lillian's mother come and take him to Kentucky with her. Then I went back out to Montana, and she joined me out there with the baby in the spring.

Q: Did you get your degree then in 1947?

Mr. Reagan: I got my degree in June--I guess it was '47. Then I got the offer to go up and play football in Canada.

Q: You told me you had an offer, also, from Chicago.

Mr. Reagan: Something called the Chicago Rockets. It was a new team.

Q: What turned you off from taking that offer?

Mr. Reagan: The contracts. The contract that was offered by the Rockets was one of those things where you could be released for little or nothing it seemed. The contract for the Canadian team was solid. I'd go there, and I'd play, and so I really think that was kind of the difference. I didn't have an attorney at that time. I was just looking and reading them over. The Chicago offer was an invitation more or less for a tryout or something, it seemed, although it was in the form of a contract to be signed for something like five grand.

But the Winnipeg Blue Bombers' contract didn't have all of the release clauses and different kinds of catches. It just seemed like a more straightforward deal. So I decided to go up there.

I think there were five of us from this country on the team: Sonnberg from Minnesota; George Smith, great big tackle from Southern; and myself; couple of others. I think they could only have five imports at that time. That was a one-year deal. I played up there, and I worked. I part-time coached a high school up there. I was ready and willing to stay, but I had my wife up there at the time. She wanted to come back to California; Canada was too cold. And, for the first time in my life, I got hurt bad enough that I had to miss a game; I missed at least three or four games. I said, "Well, maybe I'm getting too old for this stuff." So we came back down to California.

Then I worked in insurance for a while. And '49 was when Dennis got this thing together to come back for a year in recruiting in New York.

Q: What specifically do you remember from that recruiting duty?

Mr. Reagan: I went back in October '49. Then the Korean War came up in June 1950. When I began this duty, we had highly selective recruiting, and our big thing was getting qualified black people. Then we got into the recall situation, because of the Korean War.* I got busy. I mean, I got really busy because we were processing so many people there in New York every day. Many reservists were trying to get out of going back in, because everybody had just bought homes, started to work, started businesses, and families. Couples of two men were even coming in. One would be the "wife" and ask, "Am I going to get my allotment?" and all this sort of stuff, trying to get out of it that way, by pretending to be homos. So they sent a lot of those people over to the naval hospital, I guess, to find out if it was the case or not.

We were very busy signing shipping articles in addition to swearing in other regular people that were coming in.

---

*Thousands of individuals who had served on active duty in the Navy in World War II affiliated with the Naval Reserve after they returned to civilian life. When the Korean War broke out in the summer of 1950, many of these naval reservists were recalled to active duty.

Q: Was that mostly an administrative job?

Mr. Reagan: Yes.

Q: Did you get out and make public appearances and whatnot?

Mr. Reagan: Not too many. When we first came back, that was one of the things that we were to do: to try to let people again know that the services were open, and to try to get qualified black people to enlist in the Navy or go in for some of the officer programs. The work itself was a good eight-hour, nine-hour job all day long, five days a week.

Then in the fall I made some part of the East Coast recruiting trip. Then the second year I was there, I went out to the Midwest. That was for me. I was talking with Gravely, and Gravely was doing some of that too. Then I don't know what happened, but I think the third year I did it, I think it was East Coast, West Coast, and all in between that I was doing.

Q: Were you successful in getting blacks to enlist?

J. W. Reagan #2 - 208

Mr. Reagan: I think we were only minimally successful. We were going primarily to push the NROTC program. There might have been some local fallout from those visits, although there was no followup of any kind. So other than doing the PR job, I'm not so sure how successful that program was, because we never stayed around any place to follow up. So we made the trips; we gave our best pitch. In a lot of the question-and-answer sessions, there were adults in the audience who would see me up there in a lieutenant jaygee's or a lieutenant's uniform and ask me, "Can you be anything other than a mess cook in the Navy?" It just hadn't sunk in, even at that time.

Q: Well, the Navy didn't have very many black officers that you could trot out as examples.

Mr. Reagan: They didn't, that's true. But I guess it was kind of an educational job that we were trying to do, and exact numbers, I couldn't say. You know, you can talk to kids individually that would be interested in the group, and you could encourage them. And you might feel that they are probably going to be interested enough to go down and enlist or at least find out more about it. But we really didn't have a followup system on that.

Q: It sounds as if you had a real image problem to

J. W. Reagan #2 - 209

overcome, too, as far as blacks in the Navy.

Mr. Reagan: Yes, still at that time.

I think the most significant thing that happened to me was the duty with the amphibious group at the end of the Korean situation. In my secret heart I thought that the skipper would probably pick the white senior lieutenant as his exec. I think that's what I probably thought, everything being equal. But for whatever his reasons he selected me. You know, even between wars, things had changed up a little bit.

Q: Did you see other signs of progress over those six or eight years?

Mr. Reagan: You mean on the second tour?

Q: In the Navy's overall treatment of blacks.

Mr. Reagan: Well, I think so because, for whatever reason, Truman came out with the executive order on treatment of naval employees and personnel, on military bases and military situations.* I certainly think the Navy was

---

*On 26 July 1948, President Harry S Truman issued Executive Order 9981, which proclaimed, among other things, "It is hereby declared that there shall be equality of treatment and opportunity for all persons of the armed services without regard to race, color, religion, or national origin." One likely reason for the order was that Truman believed it would help in his 1948 campaign for reelection as President by getting the support of black voters.

making an effort to recruit and enlist and procure people, and a lot of this was Dennis Nelson. Again, the treatment situation, what was my experience? My experience was there in recruiting, and my personal experience was good. I never noticed any difference in treatment of recruits and reservists that we were calling back, any difference in treatment on that level.

Near the end of the war, I was sent down to Coronado, California, which had the home command for our amphibious unit, Boat Unit One. I cannot recall that there were any black enlisted men in the unit and no black officers other than myself. We went right over to Japan, around Yokosuka, Camp McGill, and I did not encounter a lot of blacks, period. I don't remember there being a black enlisted person, and there was no black officer in that group. We must have had 300 or 400 people in the whole amphibious unit, including support groups such as the frogmen and construction battalions, and all those.

Q: Were you treated with the respect due a lieutenant?

Mr. Reagan: I think so, yes. I really had no problem. The nature of the deal was a little less formal than maybe some other kinds of duties. Because when we'd get through with the day's work, we'd go to our quarters, and they'd take turns going around each other's room having cocktails

J. W. Reagan #2 - 211

or something before chow and talking and BS-ing and things like that. It was a very tight-knit type of thing as far as the officers were concerned. We had about 20 junior officers, myself, and the skipper.

We were all one big family there.

Q: Did you at that point have any idea about staying in the Navy longer?

Mr. Reagan: It was not at that point that I worried about it. See, I made lieutenant senior grade shortly after I got back, April 1950, or somewhere around there. But I apparently still had this age-in-grade problem of some kind. After that determination--whenever it was--I never concerned myself that much with it again. I suppose I may have thought about it again, if another kind of opportunity had come up.

I think what I did pass up was the chance to make up for my reserve time. Once in a while, some order comes out, if you do it by such-and-such a date. I might have been able to make up that lost time in the reserve at some point and go ahead and get my reserve retirement.

Q: Now with the age-in-grade problem, are you saying you were too old for your rank?

J. W. Reagan #2 - 212

Mr. Reagan: Yes, I was a year too old, I think.

Q: So did that mean that you didn't have the opportunity for promotion or what?

Mr. Reagan: Not for the promotion but for augmenting into the regular Navy.

Q: As you say, it's unfortunate that you didn't stick it out for the 20 years and get that retirement.

Mr. Reagan: Yes, it would have been a nice retirement check.

Q: What do you remember about the drilling and the summer cruises, or whatever time of year they were?

Mr. Reagan: I delighted in those, and they weren't all summer. Oh, gee, you got to get on the carriers, with the carrier task force, and refueling at sea and standing watches and things like that--with other officers, of course.

Q: What ships do you remember spending time in?

Mr. Reagan: I went out once on a carrier and really

experienced some exciting activity with refueling at night in rough seas and the night takeoffs and landings by the planes. Once I was on a transport, and I had a DE. I had some fine two-week duties: different places, different kinds of ships, and generally you could participate in as much watch-standing as you wanted on the bridge, CIC, and even observe the engineering watches.* I think that I did something strictly ashore once or twice, but I'm not quite sure.

Q: What was the drilling like in between the cruises at the reserve centers?

Mr. Reagan: Well, that was great. At first I had sort of an administrative job. Then I got the idea about establishing the sea cadet group, and we had a terrific little group there at Compton, California. I was spending most of my time with that, getting the kids to boot camp and drumming up uniforms from training centers and other naval activities. At that time I moved out here. This was in 1960, when Hazel and I came out here. For a while I was commuting back and forth up there, and then that got to be a bit much. Then I transferred down to San Diego. At that point I got busy again, and I didn't do the active reserve anymore. But for a while I still kept up the two-week

_____
*CIC--combat information center.

deals and the correspondence courses. Finally, I just phased out of that reserve program.

Q: What sort of civilian jobs did you have in the Fifties after you got released from active duty?

Mr. Reagan: I got out of the Navy in '54 and went to work for the state of California and got my real estate license. Then I went to USC.* Then I worked for the state a couple years, and then I started going full-time in real estate. I pretty much did that until I lost Skip. Then I went to work for the Urban League, and I worked for the Urban League for about three or four years. Then I worked for a couple years setting up the OIC program, Opportunities Industrialization Center. Then we set up this housing development corporation. And I was not quite out of real estate then, any of this, but I had these salaried jobs. And then those are the only jobs that I had, other than real estate.

Q: What was your time at USC?

Mr. Reagan: I did everything but write a thesis for a master's in public administration. I probably was there about a year, 18 months.

---
*USC--University of Southern California, Los Angeles, California.

Q: I expect there are a lot of people in that category that have everything but the thesis.

Mr. Reagan: A lot of people have done that, yes, I know.

And I think that's the main thing with those graduate degrees, that you just really need to stick to it and do it. A lot of people get the work done and don't write the thesis.

I was happy to see my stepdaughter. She got a Ph.D., and she's been teaching all the time up at Oregon State. Now she's got a job heading a department at Fresno State, so she'll be down here in California, starting this summer.*

Q: What particular area of study were you in? Did you have the thesis topic picked out that you were working on?

Mr. Reagan: I believe my interest at the time was statistical analysis in the field of economics. I can't pinpoint the topic at this date and time.

Q: Well, I'm sure that experience was valuable, though, in leading to your work with the Urban League.

---
*The stepdaughter is Sharon Elise, head of women's studies at Fresno State University, Fresno, California.

J. W. Reagan #2 - 216

Mr. Reagan: Oh, yes, it was. It was good market stuff that you got in those courses in public administration.

I think at that time I also started work with the state. Remember, I think I related those two things together quite a bit too. Because I did start with the state; I did start USC; and I did go ahead and get my license in real estate and work at it part-time.

Q: And supported a family on top of that.

Mr. Reagan: Yes, so I probably related the public administration more to work with the Department of Employment, possibly thinking in terms of a potential career in government employment of some kind.

But I think the thing that really got me serious about the real estate was that I got this deal with so many parts to it. It was for this old man that had acquired all this property, and now he was just kind of letting it fall down all around him.

Q: We talked during lunch, but not on the tape, about the experience of going to Great Lakes in 1987 for the dedication of the in-processing center named for the Golden Thirteen. What are your recollections of that?

J. W. Reagan #2 - 217

Mr. Reagan: Oh, well, now a little bit about the background of that. I'm sure maybe one of the guys or more have told you. There had been the idea of naming something after the Golden Thirteen. The Navy talked about a ship, and then there were all kinds of problems with that. Then I think the last thing that came up was that the Secretary of the Navy was looking at something at the Officer Candidate School in Newport named in honor of the Golden Thirteen. Somebody presented that to John Lehman.* I happened to see the memo, and Lehman's handwriting says, "I want something better than this for the Golden 13." How we got a copy of that memo and everything, I don't know, but it was passed to us.

I think at the time he had this in mind, because shortly thereafter, I guess Cooper or Barnes let us know that they were considering naming the new recruit in-processing center at Great Lakes in honor of the Golden Thirteen. So we thought that was a very fine and very wonderful thing to do. And then, of course, Admiral Hazard got onto it and got very interested and started making plans for it, and it just followed from there.** It was a great experience to be honored in this way.

---
*John F. Lehman, Jr., was Secretary of the Navy from 1981 to 1987.
**Rear Admiral Roberta L. Hazard, USN, was Commander Great Lakes Naval Training Center at the time the new in-processing center was dedicated in 1987.

Q: What do you remember about the ceremony itself?

Mr. Reagan: On the morning of the dedication, they had the drives leading up to the center lined with these young sailors. It was just very impressive, and we walked into the hall and we had the ribbon-cutting ceremony, and then each of us had an escort go around through the building to show us the different parts of it and everything. We just felt like real VIPs.

Q: You were indeed.

Mr. Reagan: Then they had a dance and a reception, and then the recruit graduation exercises the next day, on Saturday, and Gravely spoke. I remember Gravely putting his cane down, looking out to the center of that thing, and standing up there and talking for a half an hour. He wasn't in the best of shape at that time.

Very inspiring. And quite thrilling to have the flashback to the recruits marching in review and the different companies. It was just very impressive.

Q: Well, in a way it made more sense than something at Newport, because you had gone through your training there at Great Lakes, both boot camp and the officer training.

J. W. Reagan #2 - 219

Mr. Reagan: For an honor, what more could there be where you get recruits from all over the country going there? They have a trophy case in the center with uniform items, press releases, and all this sort of thing. We've been terrifically honored, just kind of amazing to me. I don't feel historic, but something like this kind of feels like history in the making.

Q: Well, why don't you just accept it?

Mr. Reagan: I do. I accept it. It's wonderful. I'll just admit my age and accept it.

Q: What do you remember about the trip to Scotland earlier this year?

Mr. Reagan: Now, I really think that was totally out of sight, basically because the young people did it themselves. They had the blessings of the command and everything over there, but they put the thing together.

Q: And raised the money.

Mr. Reagan: Yes, and they paid for tickets for the whole group of us--not for the wives, of course--but just to get that much done and to set aside a whole program like that, and to have us escorted around by a couple of master chiefs for a week. You know, that's money too. But I think of all the honors, that was the most touching because of the way the individual sailors in the command dug in their pockets, or whatever they did--car washes and whatever else they did. They treated us so, so graciously, all of them, I mean the officers and the crew. It was just really outstanding. It just moved me very much because they did it themselves.

Q: What sort of program or festivities did they have?

Mr. Reagan: We were involved in a change of command ceremony. Some of us had lunch in the chiefs' mess, some of us in the enlisted quarters. What they were celebrating, basically, was Black History Month. They had the big banquet and the affair on Sunday, February 26, I guess it was, all kinds of soul food, home cooking there, and some good gospel music. We attended the chiefs' ball, and we were honored there with the chiefs. Then, of course, we had a couple trips out to Glasgow and Edinburgh. We were just busy all the time that we were there touring; we had a tour of the ship. Then we had the new deputy commander NavEur.* There was a young guy that was very impressive. There was a vice admiral that was a flier and

_____
*NavEur--U.S. Naval Forces Europe.

a certified Vietnam hero.* He got shot down, chopped his way out of the jungle Rambo-style, they described it. And so we got to hear him speak at the change of command. We just had a wonderful round of activity.

Then we had a session that we sponsored with some refreshments and things to invite the enlisted people, and anybody that wanted to come, you know, and talk and things of this kind.

Q: Do you have any recollections of individual encounters with the sailors that are especially interesting?

Mr. Reagan: There were a lot of them. The most interesting guy would be, I guess, my typical chief, Master Chief Robert E. Lee, who was the master chief for the Simon Lake. What a character! I guess he's about to retire, but he's from the South and his father was from the South-- well, his whole family was. We stayed in the home of the exec and his wife and Bob Lee and his wife, and George and Peggy Cooper stayed with them. We were all there at sort of an after party. He was telling me about how his dad left the South because he was disgusted with the race setup, and didn't want to have any part of it. They had an inheritance there, and his father made him promise that he

---
*Vice Admiral Edward H. Martin, USN, Deputy Commander in Chief U.S. Naval Forces Europe, was a prisoner of war during the Vietnam War.

would have nothing to do with racial discrimination. And I said, "Well, you know, that might be fine, but maybe you ought to go back and claim your inheritance."

He said, "I don't know whether I can, because I promised him I wouldn't." But, anyway, he would be my vote for a prototype Navy master chief. Just his manner and his take-charge attitude and that sort of thing. I was very impressed with him.

We had some talks with some young people who were concerned about their careers, both enlisted and a couple young officers, black officers, ensigns, who wanted to know where they go from here. Specifically what I could tell them was to figure out, "What's your goal, where do you want to go? Then you may have to network, maybe connect with the NNOA or some more senior types, or even challenge some people here, your senior type people here. You know, don't be afraid to go up and find out. But know yourself where you want to go, and, also, find out about the career structure and, you know, if you really want to stay in and advance, you're going to have to have so much sea time, so much different kinds of duties and things of that type. Stay away from the things that are going to kill you, you know. And just don't be afraid to go for it."

A lot of people just wanted to know how it was when we were coming along. Then they would tell you how proud they are of you. And you, of course, and sincerely so, you tell them how proud you feel about them.

So we had quite a lot of that, and I guess that was one of the purposes of our coming over there. They're anxious to do it again next year. I said, "I don't know how you do it."

Then the chiefs got together and said, "Well, we think you ought to visit more commands than one." So I don't know what they're cooking up. The <u>Simon Lake</u> had maybe 1,200, 1,400 people. About 400 of them were female, and I guess maybe almost half the crew was black. And I suppose in all of the commands--I don't know how far you can stretch them out, but I suppose all the commands overseas have probably a representative number of blacks and females. And it seems to be working out fine.

Q: Sounds as if you have a continuing job.

Mr. Reagan: Yes, really, really. I was very unhappy that Graham Martin couldn't see that, despite the fact it was an exceptional honor paid to us.*

Q: Well, I guess as a final question: what do you see as a continuing role for the Golden Thirteen?

---

*Because of the physical condition of Golden Thirteen member Graham Martin and his wife Alma, they were unable to undertake the long journey to Scotland in early 1989.

J. W. Reagan #2 - 224

Mr. Reagan: Well, I'm not sure at this stage of the game that we can go out and bring in a significant number of recruits or if that's the thing. But I know what we certainly can do. We all love the Navy, and I think we all promote the Navy and the naval services at every opportunity. Some of us are a lot more active and more involved than others, but I think we appreciate the Navy; we appreciate the people in it; we appreciate all the honors that they've paid us. And I would say this, I don't know what we can do in a specific way for the Navy, but I'll tell you, we'll do everything that we can. If we're called upon, I think we're all just extremely willing and ready and able to go out and do everything that we can for Navy programs.

I'm looking forward again, because we missed them last year because of the dedication, to meeting with the NNOA at Long Beach this year. I missed seeing all of those large numbers of young officers. I hope that the individual young officers now would take it upon themselves to continue their Navy careers and keep it going, because it's really been wonderful to me to see skippers of carriers, wing commanders, base commanders, all those types. They're just spread out thin, but they're almost in every level of activity in the Navy, and every rank up through admiral. I don't know how many people are in the pipeline for what, but I would like to see them keep it going. I think it would be good for the Navy, good for the country.

Q: Speaking of honors, it's an honor for me to have the association with the group, the Golden Thirteen, and to have the opportunity to record your stories. I'm very grateful to you for making that contribution.

Mr. Reagan: Thank you very much, Paul. We certainly appreciate the work and the job you're doing with the interviews. I don't envy you putting this stuff together, because I know at this stage of the game, we old guys tend to ramble a lot, but when it comes back it seems like it's all together.

Q: Well, I enjoy it, so it's a pleasant job.

Mr. Reagan: Well, thank you very much.

Q: Thank you.

Index to
Reminiscences of John W. Reagan

Accidents
    Two people were lost during the operation of a yard tugboat commanded by Reagan near the end of World War II, 194-195

Alves, A.
    Speculation as to why he wasn't selected as a black commissioned officer at close of Great Lakes training in early 1944, 40, 191

"Amos and Andy"
    Racially biased radio comedy program in the 1930s that Reagan's family considered hilarious, 16-17

Amphibious Warfare
    Reagan served in an amphibious boat unit in Coronado, California, and Japan during the latter part of the Korean War, 72-75, 174-176, 209

Anderson, Marian
    Concert singer who appeared at the Hampton Naval Training School in Virginia in 1943, 168-169

Arbor, Jesse W.
    Golden Thirteen member who was a good athlete, 24; jovial storyteller and morale booster during group training in 1944, 44-45, 182

Armstrong, Commander Daniel W., USNR (USNA, 1915)
    Reagan had little contact with this officer in charge of Camp Robert Smalls at Great Lakes, Illinois, in early 1944, 32-33, 176-177; criticized by Golden Thirteen member Dennis D. Nelson, 32-33

Army Air Corps, U.S.
    Reagan was recruited by in 1940 and 1941, 19-21, 26; Reagan just missed an opportunity to train with the 99th Pursuit Squadron, 19-20, 158-159

Athletics
    Reagan's pronounced abilities from adolescence onward, 5, 10; Reagan played college football at Montana State University in the 1940s, 6, 10, 22-23, 66-67, 69-71, 138-140; Reagan was a professional football player in Canada in 1947, 23-24, 67-69, 204-205; Reagan was involved in

the construction of a slab for sports on Okinawa in 1945, 64-65; Reagan was an excellent wrestler in both high school and college, 71, 134-136; he was also a track man in high school, 137; enlisted men ran obstacle course at Great Lakes, Illinois, during recruit training in 1942, 157-158

Barnes, Phillip G.
Serious, studious member of the first class of black naval officers trained at Great Lakes, Illinois, in early 1944, 45, 57

Barnes, Dr. Samuel E.
Golden Thirteen member who was a good athlete, 24; father-confessor type who demonstrated a wry sense of humor during officer training in early 1944, 45-46

Baugh, Dalton L.
Golden Thirteen member who was a good athlete, 24; trained at Hampton, Virginia, before going to Great Lakes, Illinois, for officer training in early 1944, 29; brilliant man with a great deal of common sense, 46-47, 152-153

Black Naval Officers
See Golden Thirteen; National Naval Officers Association

Boy Scouts
Reagan participated in the program in the Chicago area in the 1930s, 13-14

Brown, Midshipman Wesley A., Jr. (USNA, 1949)
Surprised, as first black graduate of the U.S. Naval Academy, by various types of prejudice there, 8-9

Camp Robert Smalls
Segregated training site for black recruits within the Great Lakes Naval Training Station in World War II, 8, 186-187; Reagan was an apprentice chief petty officer of the company, 24-27, 155-158, 162; facilities for black officer candidates in early 1944, 31-32; curriculum and testing at, 34-35, 41-42; typical day at, 37; liberty and family visitation at, 38; highlights of training, 39; thorough screening of all candidates, 40-41

Communism
    Reagan did not fall under its influence in black communities during the 1930s, 17-18, 41, 104-105, 116-118

Cooper, George C.
    Golden Thirteen member who was an instructor at Hampton, Virginia, during World War II, 29-30; dignified, mature, analytical, well-organized member of the group of black enlisted men training in 1944 to be officers, 47-48, 57; returned to duty at Hampton, Virginia, following commissioning in 1944, 193-194

Depression
    Effects upon Reagan's family in the 1930s, 2-3

Dille, Lieutenant (junior grade) John F., Jr., USNR
    Reserve officer who was very supportive of the members of the Golden Thirteen while they were going through officer training in early 1944, 178

Downes, Commander Edwin H., USNR (USNA, 1920)
    As officer in charge of the naval training school at Hampton, Virginia, told Reagan in late 1943 that he would be going to Great Lakes, Illinois, for a special assignment, 27-28, 167; had an impressive knowledge of the men in his battalion at Hampton, 29; recommended several men for inclusion in first training course for black officers, 30; demonstrated excellent leadership qualities, 165-167; relationship changed after Reagan was commissioned in 1944, 193

Education
    Reagan's elementary and secondary training in Chicago in the 1930s, 5-6, 128-129; studies at Montana State University before and after World War II, 6, 10, 21-23, 66-67, 140-142; Dennis Nelson ran a remedial reading program for black sailors at Great Lakes, Illinois, during World War II, 187; literacy instruction for black people in the society of the 1980s, 187-189

FBI
    See Federal Bureau of Investigation

Federal Bureau of Investigation
Investigated prospective black officer candidates before they were selected for training at Great Lakes, Illinois, in early 1944, 185-186

Fessenden, Douglas A.
Head football coach at Montana State University in the 1930s and 1940s for whom Reagan played, 10, 66, 140, 204

Football
Reagan played for Coach Doug Fessenden at Montana State University both before and after his service in World War II, 10, 22-23, 66-67, 69-71, 138-140; Reagan played professional football in Canada in 1947, 23-24, 67-69, 204-205

Firefly (Auxiliary Minesweeper)
Small ship in which Reagan served in 1943 during operations out of San Diego, 163-164, 170-173

Golden Thirteen
Many of this first class of black naval officers were good athletes, 24; officer training at Great Lakes, Illinois, in early 1944, 31-43, 51, 178-187; members of the Golden Thirteen were not permitted to use the officers' club after their commissioning, 33, 59-60, 201-202; sense of vision and purpose throughout their training, 36-37; assessments of individual members of the group, 44-57; deep sense of pride among members, 54; reunions of the group in the 1970s and 1980s, 83-86; the title did not originate within the group, 150-151; the group generally got disappointing assignments after being commissioned, 173-175; satisfaction from commissioning in March 1944, 189-190; three members of the group that went through training did not become officers, 190-192; a building at the Great Lakes Naval Training Center was named in honor of the group in 1987, 217-219; surviving members of the group were honored by the crew of the submarine tender Simon Lake (AS-33) in Scotland in early 1989, 219-223

Goodwin, Reginald E.
Golden Thirteen member who was the liaison between the officer candidates and Commander Daniel W. Armstrong during training at Great Lakes, Illinois, in early 1944, 32-33; group disciplinarian, 49, 181-182

Gravely, Vice Admiral Samuel L., Jr., USN (Ret.)
Trained and served at Hampton, Virginia, during World War II, 30; Reagan's admiration for Gravely's achievement of fleet-commander status in the 1970s, 36-37; served in San Diego in 1943 and spent time with Reagan, 171; spoke at the 1987 dedication of a building at Great Lakes, Illinois, named in honor of the Golden Thirteen, 218

Great Lakes (Illinois) Naval Training Center
The in-processing building at the training center was named in honor of the Golden Thirteen in 1987, 217-219

Great Lakes (Illinois) Naval Training Station
Location of recruit training for Reagan in 1942, 24-27, 155-158, 162; one of two main sources from which black officer candidates were chosen, 29; facilities for black officer candidates in early 1944, 31-32; members of the Golden Thirteen were not permitted to use the officers' club after their 1944 commissioning, 33, 59-60, 201-202; curriculum and testing at, 34-35, 41-42; typical day at, 37; liberty and family visitation at, 38; highlights of training, 39, 178-187; thorough screening of all candidates, 40-41

Hair, James E.
Member of the Golden Thirteen who has been active in community affairs in his retirement, 49; excellent ship handler and an individual whose disposition was cheery, calm, and good humored, 50-51; reunited with other members of the Golden Thirteen on board the USS Kidd (DDG-993) in 1982, 85-86; demonstrated strong leadership qualities as skipper of a yard tugboat late in World War II, 196-197

Hampton (Virginia) Naval Training School
Operated segregated class A service school for blacks in World War II, 8, 27-28, 58-59, 162-170, 192-193; where Reagan met his first wife, 26; one of two main sources from which black officer candidates were chosen in 1943, 29

Integration
See Racial Integration

Kidd, USS (DDG-993)
    Guided missile destroyer that was the site of a reunion of the Golden Thirteen in 1982, 85-86

Korean War
    Recruiters aided in the process of recalling reservists to active duty in 1950 to take part in the war, 73, 206-209; Reagan served in an amphibious boat unit in Coronado, California, and Japan during the latter part of the war, 72-75, 174-176

Labor Unions
    Reagan became involved in organizing a union shop at a meat-packing plant in Illinois in the early 1940s, 117-118, 130-131

Lear, Charles B.
    Golden Thirteen member who thoroughly loved the Navy and urgently desired to be a permanent part of it, committed suicide after World War II, 51-53

Lehman, John
    Secretary of the Navy in the 1980s who was involved in the naming of a building at the Great Lakes Naval Training Center in honor of the Golden Thirteen, 217

Logistics
    Reagan worked with a black logistics support company on Guam and Okinawa near the end of World War II, 63-65, 201, 203

Marine Corps, U.S.
    Reagan's only son was killed while serving with the Marine Corps in Vietnam in the 1960s, 159-161

Martin, Graham E.
    Golden Thirteen member who was a good athlete and deeply religious, 53-54

Montana State University
    Reagan studied and played football at the university both before and after his participation in World War II, 6-7, 21-23, 66-67, 69-71, 118, 138-142; small cell of Communists existed on the campus in the 1940s, 118; Reagan was involved in the ROTC program, 153-155

National Naval Officers Association
    Black naval officers as a group have made many advances in the 1980s, 83-85; competing within the system for promotions in the 1980s, 88-89, 222-224

Naval Reserve
    Reagan's experiences as a reservist in the 1950s while drilling and on training duty, 212-214

Naval Training School, Hampton, Virginia
    See Hampton (Virginia) Naval Training School

Naval Training Station, Great Lakes, Illinois
    See Great Lakes (Illinois) Naval Training Station

Nelson, Dennis D. II
    Golden Thirteen member who felt negatively toward the officer in charge of Camp Robert Smalls, Commander Daniel W. Armstrong, during officer training in 1944, 32-33; prolific storyteller who amused fellow officer candidates, 44-45; deep sense of pride in being part of the Navy, 52, 54-55; got Reagan recalled to active duty in late 1949 to help recruit blacks, 72, 205, 209-210; various contacts with Reagan over the years, 76-77, 109, 145-147; aspects of personality, 147-150; ran a remedial reading program for black sailors at Great Lakes, Illinois, during World War II, 187

New York City
    Reagan's service time around the city in 1944-45 involved meeting many black celebrities of the era, 62-63

Norfolk, Virginia
    Reagan was the victim of racial discrimination by a bus driver while serving in the Norfolk area during World War II, 7; segregated ferryboat between Norfolk and Hampton during World War II, 114-115

Okinawa
    Reagan recommended building a big concrete slab for the recreation of Navy personnel serving on the island in 1945, 64-65

Oxnard, California
   Reagan was the victim of racial discrimination by a restaurant while serving in the area during World War II, 7-8, 202-203

Payton, Chief Petty Officer Noble
   Extremely articulate, suave black instructor who impressed Reagan at Camp Robert Smalls during the training of the first black naval officers in 1944, 43, 178-179

Racial Integration
   Reagan's elementary and secondary education in integrated Chicago schools in the 1920s and 1930s, 6; Reagan served in an integrated amphibious boat unit during the Korean War and was chosen as executive officer over a white competitor, 73-74, 174-176, 209; increased opportunities for blacks in the Navy by the time of the Korean War, 209-211

Racial Prejudice
   Reagan's earliest perception of it as a child in Texas, 6; scattered incidents of in such disparate locations as Montana, Texas, Virginia, and California, 6-8, 82, 113-116, 138, 202-203; absence of at Camp Robert Smalls, 33; preparation for the bias of white officers, 35

Racial Segregation
   Within the U.S. Navy in the 1940s, 8, 186-187; at Great Lakes, Illinois in early 1944, members of the Golden Thirteen were not permitted to use the officers' club after their commissioning, 33, 59-60, 201-202; various incidents experienced by Reagan over the years, 113-116, 169-170

Reagan, Bernice
   The mother of John W. Reagan, she worked in the 1930s and 1940s as a domestic to help support her family, 3-4, 96, 121; had several separations from her husband over the years, 3, 91-95; influence on her son's development, 9, 11-13, 98-99, 101-102, 105-106, 112; Reagan visited with her while on duty in California in 1943, 171

Reagan, John L.
   The father of John W. Reagan, he worked in a variety of jobs in the 1930s and 1940s, 2, 14-15, 124, 126; had

several separations from his wife over the years, 3, 91-95; influence on his son's development, 13, 96-98, 102-103; had a very conservative political philosophy, 103-105; 120-122

Reagan, John W.
Childhood memories from 1920s and 1930s, 1-5, 15-16, 100-101, 122-128; parents' personalities and influence on Reagan, 2-4, 9, 11-12, 14-15, 91-99, 101-106, 112; siblings of, 3, 93, 98, 106, 122, 128; aspired to be an entertainer, 5, 9, 127; studied and played football at Montana State University both before and after his participation in World War II, 6-7, 21-23, 66-67, 69-71, 138-142; high school experiences in the late 1930s, 5, 11, 13-14, 128-129; jobs during teen years in the 1930s, 14-15; enlistment in the Navy in 1942 after expressing a preference for the Army Air Corps, 19-21, 24-26; recruit training at Great Lakes, Illinois, in 1942, 24-27, 155-158, 162; trained as an electrician's mate in Hampton, Virginia, and served as battalion commander Frank E. Sublett Jr.'s adjutant, 27-31, 162-170; underwent officer training at Great Lakes, Illinois, in early 1944, 31-58, 178-187; served in the Korean War, 55 achieved rank of lieutenant commander in the reserves, 55-56; first set of orders after commissioning were to Hampton Institute with Sublett, 58-59, 192-193; first wife Lillian, 60, 68, 143-145, 159, 168, 170, 203-204; duty in yard tug in the New York area with James Hair during 1944-45, 60-63, 194-197, 199-200; worked with a black logistics support company on Guam and Okinawa near the end of World War II, 63-65, 201, 203; children of, 66, 143, 159-161; played professional football in Canada in 1947, 67-69, 204-205; served as a Navy recruiter in New York City at the beginning of the Korean War, 72-73, 206-210; Reagan served in an amphibious boat unit during the latter part of the Korean War, 72-75, 174-176, 210-211; work in real estate and state government following the conclusion of naval service, 77-78, 107-112, 132-134, 214-216; held several jobs for the Urban League in Los Angeles, 77-80, 109, 132; involvement in Navy recruiting in the 1980s, 87; job in Illiois meat-packing plant in the early 1940s, 117-118, 130-131; leadership qualities, 131-133; Reagan was an excellent wrestler in high school in Illinois in the 1930s, 134-136; second wife Hazel, 151-152; duty in auxiliary minesweeper <u>Firefly</u> operating out of San Diego

in 1943, 170-173; satisfaction of being commissioned an officer in 1944, 189-190; commanded a patrol craft in 1944, 197-198; Naval Reserve experiences in the 1950s while not on active duty, 212-214

Reagan, John W., Jr
Birth of Reagan's only son in March 1946, 66, 203-204; killed while serving in Vietnam in the 1960s, 159-161

Recruiting
Reagan and others were recalled to active duty in the late 1940s to facilitate recruiting blacks into the Navy, 72-73, 206-209; Reagan's work in Navy recruiting in the 1980s, 87

Recruit Training
Reagan underwent boot camp training at Great Lakes, Illinois, in 1942, 24-27, 155-158, 162

Religion
Its place in Reagan's parents' lives, 12; Reagan describes himself as a searcher, 12

Reserve Officers Training Corps (ROTC)
Reagan's ROTC experience at Montana State University around 1940 prepared him to be a company leader while at Navy boot camp, 24-25, 153-155

Robeson, Paul
Reagan's brief meeting with this actor and athlete in Butte, Montana, in the 1940s, 18, 118-119

Roosevelt, Franklin D.
President who was well liked in the black community in the 1930s because he gave some promise of relief from the Depression, 119-120

Rymkus, Louis
Future professional football player against whom Reagan wrestled in high school in the late 1930s, 134-135

Scotland
The submarine tender Simon Lake (AS-33) played host to the Coopers for Black History Month while deployed to Holy Loch in February 1988, 219-223

Segregation
   See Racial Segregation

Simon Lake, USS (AS-33)
   Submarine tender whose crew raised money for a visit by surviving members of the Golden Thirteen in early 1989, 219-223

Sublett, Frank E., Jr.
   Golden Thirteen member who was a good athlete at the University of Wisconsin, 24; battalion commander at Hampton, Virginia, in 1943, 27-31, 144, 168; great friend of Reagan's, 56; first set of orders after commissioning were to Hampton Institute with Reagan, 58-59; similarities to Reagan, 144-145, 161, 184-185

Training
   Reagan's time at Great Lakes, Illinois, boot camp in 1942, 24-27, 155-158, 162; the Navy operated a service school for training black enlisted men at Hampton, Virginia, in World War II, 27, 162-170, 192-193; officer training for black enlisted men at Great Lakes, Illinois, in early 1944, 31-43, 51, 178-187; Reagan served in an amphibious boat unit that was involved in training during the Korean War, 74-75

Urban League
   Work in the Los Angeles area in the 1960s and 1970s to promote black interests, 77-80, 187-188

Vietnam War
   Reagan's only son was killed while serving with the Marine Corps in Vietnam in the 1960s, 159-161

White, William Sylvester
   Golden Thirteen member who bears the quiet, meditative, and analytical personality of a judge, 56-57

Williams, Lewis R.
   Speculation as to why he wasn't selected as a black commissioned officer at close of Great Lakes training in 1944, 40

Wrestling
   Reagan was an excellent wrestler in high school in Illinois in the 1930s, 134-136